First World War
and Army of Occupation
War Diary
France, Belgium and Germany

40 DIVISION
121 Infantry Brigade
Alexandra, Princess of Wales's Own (Yorkshire Regiment)
13th Battalion
27 May 1916 - 31 July 1918

WO95/2616/2

The Naval & Military Press Ltd
www.nmarchive.com
Published in association with The National Archives

Published by

The Naval & Military Press Ltd

Unit 10 Ridgewood Industrial Park,

Uckfield, East Sussex,

TN22 5QE England

Tel: +44 (0) 1825 749494

www.naval-military-press.com

www.nmarchive.com

This diary has been reprinted in facsimile from the original. Any imperfections are inevitably reproduced and the quality may fall short of modern type and cartographic standards.

© Crown Copyright
Images reproduced by permission of The National Archives, London, England, 2015.

Contents

Document type	Place/Title	Date From	Date To
Miscellaneous	WO95/2616/2		
Heading	40th Division 121st Infy Bde 13th Bn Yorkshire Regt Jun 1916-Jly 1918		
Heading	War Diary of 13th (S) Battalion Yorkshire Regiment. from 1st July, 1916 to 31st July, 1916 (Volume 2)		
War Diary	Woking	27/05/1916	04/06/1916
War Diary	Soulthampton	05/06/1916	05/06/1916
War Diary	Le Havre France	06/06/1916	06/06/1916
War Diary	Ham-en-Artois	07/06/1916	12/06/1916
War Diary	Maumit-le-Ruitz	19/06/1916	28/06/1916
War Diary	Calonne	29/06/1916	30/06/1916
Miscellaneous	13th (Service) Battalion Yorkshire Regt.		
War Diary	Calonne.	01/07/1916	02/07/1916
War Diary	Maishil Les Ruitz	03/07/1916	03/07/1916
War Diary	Maroc	04/07/1916	10/07/1916
War Diary	Les-Brebis	11/07/1916	16/07/1916
War Diary	Maroc	17/07/1916	29/07/1916
War Diary	No. 1 Sub Sector Loos	29/07/1916	31/07/1916
Heading	War Diary of 13th (Service) Battalion Yorkshire Regiment from 1st August 1916 to 31st August 1916 (Volume 3)		
War Diary	Maroc.	01/08/1916	04/08/1916
War Diary	Les Brebis	05/08/1916	11/08/1916
War Diary	Maroc	12/08/1916	31/08/1916
Heading	War Diary of 13th Service Battalion Yorkshire Regiment from 1st September 1916 to 31st September 1916 Volume 4		
War Diary	Maroc	01/09/1916	05/09/1916
War Diary	Les Brebis	06/09/1916	09/09/1916
War Diary	Prevere Passage Loos	11/09/1916	14/09/1916
War Diary	Maroc	15/09/1916	17/09/1916
War Diary	Loos	19/09/1916	28/09/1916
War Diary	Prewike Passage Loos	30/09/1916	30/09/1916
Heading	War Diary of 13th (Service) Battalion Yorkshire Regiment from 1st October 1916 to 31st October 1916 (Volume 5)		
War Diary	Maroc.	01/10/1916	03/10/1916
War Diary	Loos	04/10/1916	12/10/1916
War Diary	Mazingarbe	13/10/1916	20/10/1916
War Diary	14 Bis	21/10/1916	26/10/1916
War Diary	Les Brebis	27/10/1916	28/10/1916
War Diary	Bruay	29/10/1916	29/10/1916
War Diary	Villers Brulin	29/10/1916	31/10/1916
Heading	War Diary of 13th (Service) Battalion Yorkshire Regiment from 1st November 1916 to 30th November 1916 (Volume 6)		
War Diary	Villers-Brulin	01/11/1916	01/11/1916
War Diary	Rosiere	02/11/1916	03/11/1916
War Diary	Neuvillette	04/11/1916	04/11/1916
War Diary	Candas	05/11/1916	14/11/1916

War Diary	Villers-L'Hopital	15/11/1916	16/11/1916
War Diary	Neuvillette	17/11/1916	17/11/1916
War Diary	Sus-St-Leger	18/11/1916	21/11/1916
War Diary	Doullens	22/11/1916	22/11/1916
War Diary	Berteaucourt-Les-Dames	23/11/1916	23/11/1916
War Diary	Franlieres	24/11/1916	24/11/1916
War Diary	Villers-Sous-Ailly	25/11/1916	30/11/1916
Heading	War Diary of 13th (S) Battalion Yorkshire Regiment. From 1st December 1916 To 31st December 1916 (Volume 7)		
War Diary	Villers Sous Ailly	01/12/1916	10/12/1916
War Diary	Sailly Laurette	11/12/1916	26/12/1916
War Diary	Suzanne Camp 17	27/12/1916	30/12/1916
War Diary	A.23.d A2 Bert Map.	31/12/1916	31/12/1916
Heading	War Diary of 13th (S) Battalion Yorkshire Regiment From 1st January 1917 To 31st January 1917 (Volume 8)		
War Diary	A.23.D. Albert Map	01/01/1917	01/01/1917
War Diary	Bouchavesnes North	05/01/1917	08/01/1917
War Diary	Camp 17 Suzanne	09/01/1917	09/01/1917
War Diary	Rancourt Albany	12/01/1917	12/01/1917
War Diary	Rancourt.	16/01/1917	20/01/1917
War Diary	Maurepas Ravine	21/01/1917	21/01/1917
War Diary	Camp 17 Suzanne	22/01/1917	22/01/1917
War Diary	Camp 13	25/01/1917	25/01/1917
War Diary	Bray	27/01/1917	31/01/1917
Heading	War Diary of 13th (S) Battalion Yorkshire Regiment From 1st February 1917. To 28th February 1917 (Volume 9)		
War Diary	Bray	01/02/1917	10/02/1917
War Diary	Camp 21	11/02/1917	11/02/1917
War Diary	Albany	21/02/1917	21/02/1917
War Diary	Rancourt	22/02/1917	24/02/1917
War Diary	Albany	25/02/1917	27/02/1917
War Diary	Rancourt	28/02/1917	28/02/1917
Heading	War Diary of 13th (S) Battalion Yorkshire Regiment. From 1st March 1917 To 31st March 1917 (Volume 10)		
War Diary	Rancourt	01/03/1917	04/03/1917
War Diary	Maurepas Ravine	05/03/1917	05/03/1917
War Diary	Linger Camp	06/03/1917	14/03/1917
War Diary	Clery R Sector	15/03/1917	18/03/1917
War Diary	Clery Sur Somme	14/03/1917	20/03/1917
War Diary	La Quinconce	21/03/1917	24/03/1917
War Diary	Feuillaucourt	25/03/1917	31/03/1917
Heading	War Diary of 13th (S) Battn Yorkshire Regiment. From. April 1st 1917 To April 30th 1917 Volume 11		
War Diary	Feuillaucourt	01/04/1917	04/04/1917
War Diary	Manancourt	05/04/1917	05/04/1917
War Diary	Ref 57.e.S.E W.3.4.9	06/04/1917	11/04/1917
War Diary	Fins.	12/04/1917	13/04/1917
War Diary	Elhcourt.	24/04/1917	24/04/1917
War Diary	Villers Plouich	25/04/1917	28/04/1917
Heading	War Diary of 13th (S) Battalion Yorkshire Regiment From May 1st 1917 To May 31st 1917 (Volume 12)		
War Diary	Fins & Desalt Wood	13/04/1917	13/04/1917
War Diary	Desart Wood	14/04/1917	19/04/1917

War Diary	Erricourt.	20/04/1917	24/04/1917
War Diary	Villers Plouich	24/04/1917	30/04/1917
War Diary	Map Ref France 57.c.S.E Villere Plouich	01/05/1917	01/05/1917
War Diary	Desart Wood	02/05/1917	06/05/1917
War Diary	Villers Plouich	07/05/1917	13/05/1917
War Diary	Sofez Le Grand	14/05/1917	22/05/1917
War Diary	Desart Wood	23/05/1917	25/05/1917
War Diary	Villers Plouich	25/05/1917	31/05/1917
Heading	War Diary of 13th (S) Battalion Yorkshire Regiment From June 1st 1917 To June 30th 1917 (Volume 13)		
War Diary	Villers-Plouich	01/06/1917	02/06/1917
War Diary	Sorel-Le-Grand	03/06/1917	10/06/1917
War Diary	Gonnelieu Sector W.H.a. Map 5/c S.E. 1/20000	11/06/1917	18/06/1917
War Diary	Gonnelieu Right Sub Sector	19/06/1917	26/06/1917
War Diary	Fins	27/06/1917	30/06/1917
Heading	War Diary of 13th (S) Battalion Yorkshire Regiment From July 1st 1917 To July 31st 1917 (Volume 14)		
War Diary	Fins	01/07/1917	01/07/1917
War Diary	X.3.d.b.3. Ref Map 5/c SE Scale 1/00.000. Villers-Guislain	02/07/1917	02/07/1917
War Diary	Villers-Guislain Ref Sheet 5/c SE Scale 1/20000 X9.d.5.1	02/07/1917	03/07/1917
War Diary	Villers-Guislain X.9.d.5.1.	04/07/1917	10/07/1917
War Diary	Villers-Guislain X.3.d.6.3.	11/07/1917	15/07/1917
War Diary	Vaucellette Farm	16/07/1917	17/07/1917
War Diary	Villers-Guislain X.9.d.5.1.	18/07/1917	31/07/1917
Heading	War Diary of 13th (S) Battn. Yorkshire Regt. From 1st August 1917 To 31st August 1917 (Volume 15)		
War Diary	Ref Map. 5/c S.E. Scale 1.20000. X.9.d.5.1 Villers-Guislan	01/08/1917	01/08/1917
War Diary	Poppy Post Cemetery Road. X.2.b.7.1	02/08/1917	05/08/1917
War Diary	Vaucellette Farm	06/08/1917	11/08/1917
War Diary	Gonnelieu R.26.d.40.80.	11/08/1917	18/08/1917
War Diary	Poppy Post Cemetery Road X.2.b.7.1	19/08/1917	22/08/1917
War Diary	Vaucellette Farm.	23/08/1917	27/08/1917
War Diary	Gonnelieu R.26.d.40.30	27/08/1917	31/08/1917
Heading	War Diary of 13th (S) Battn. Yorkshire Regiment. From 1st. September 1917 To 30th. September 1917 (Volume 16)		
War Diary	Ref. Map 27 S.E. Gonnelieu R.26.d.40.80.	01/09/1917	04/09/1917
War Diary	Cross Post Cemetery Road X.26.80.10	04/09/1917	08/09/1917
War Diary	Cross Post Cemetery Road	04/09/1917	08/09/1917
War Diary	Vaucellette Farm. X.13.c.3.3.	08/09/1917	12/09/1917
War Diary	Gonnelien 9.26.d.40.80	12/09/1917	23/09/1917
War Diary	Cross Post Cemetery Road	23/09/1917	27/09/1917
War Diary	Vaucellette Farm. X.13.c.3.3	27/09/1917	30/09/1917
Miscellaneous	13th Service Battalion Yorkshire Regiment		
Heading	War Diary of 13th (Service) Battalion Yorkshire Regt. From 1st October 1917 to 31st October 1917		
War Diary	Ref. Map. 57c. S.E. Scale 1/10,000 Gonnelieu R.26.d.20.80	01/10/1917	08/10/1917
War Diary	Hut Railton W.16.c.	09/10/1917	09/10/1917
War Diary	Geromne.	10/10/1917	10/10/1917
War Diary	Barky 51c 1/40.000	10/10/1917	10/10/1917
War Diary	Sus. St Leger 51 C. 1/40,000	29/10/1917	31/10/1917

Heading	War Diary of 13th (Service) Battn Yorkshire Regiment From 1st November 1917 To 30th November 1917 (Volume 13)		
War Diary	Sus St. Leger	01/11/1917	15/11/1917
War Diary	Barly 51c 1/40.000	16/11/1917	16/11/1917
War Diary	Achiet-Le-Petit 51c 1/40,000	17/11/1917	18/11/1917
War Diary	Rocquigny 51c 1/40.000	19/11/1917	20/11/1917
War Diary	Beaumetz-Les-Cambria 51c 1/40.000	21/11/1917	21/11/1917
War Diary	Sugar Factory E 29 a Moeuvres Special Sheet 1/20,000	22/11/1917	24/11/1917
War Diary	K.16.c.8.7	25/11/1917	25/11/1917
War Diary	Bertincourt. Lens II. No 1 1/10000	26/11/1917	27/11/1917
Heading	War Diary of 13th (Service) Battalion Yorkshire Regiment From 1st December 1917 To 31st December 1917 (Volume19)		
War Diary	Bellacourt Rens II Map 1/100,000	01/12/1917	01/12/1917
War Diary	Ervillers 51c 1/40,000 T.22.d.8.9. Bullecourt Map 1/10,000	02/12/1917	09/12/1917
War Diary	T.22.d.29 Bullecourt Map 1/10000	02/12/1917	09/12/1917
War Diary	Ervillers	10/12/1917	17/12/1917
War Diary	Lincoln Support	18/12/1917	23/12/1917
War Diary	Ervillers	24/12/1917	26/12/1917
War Diary	H.2b.8.1	27/12/1917	31/12/1917
War Diary	U.260.8.1 Ref 51b SW 57c N.W. 1/20,000	27/12/1917	31/12/1917
Heading	War Diary of 13th (Service) Battalion Yorkshire Regiment from 1st January 1918 to 31st January 1918 (Volume 20)		
War Diary	U.28.c.9.3 Ref Map Special Sheet U.1. To C.6. Scale 1/10,000	01/01/1918	04/01/1918
War Diary	L'Abbaye Mory	05/01/1918	08/01/1918
War Diary	U.28c.9.3 Ref Map Special Sheet U.1. To C.6 Scale 1/10,000	08/01/1918	12/01/1918
War Diary	U.26.c.7.1 Ref. Map Special Sheet UI To C.6. Scale 1/10,000	12/01/1918	16/01/1918
War Diary	U.28.c.9.3. Ref Maps Spec Sheet U1 To C B Scale 1/10.000	16/01/1918	20/01/1918
War Diary	L'Abbaye Mory	20/01/1918	24/01/1918
War Diary	U.28.c.9.3 Ref Map Special Sh U.1 To C.6 Scale 1/10,000	24/01/1918	28/01/1918
War Diary	U.26.c.7.31 Ref Map Spec Sheet U.1 to c.6 Scale 1/10,000	24/01/1918	31/01/1918
Heading	War Diary of 13th (Service) Battalion Yorkshire Regiment From 1st February 1918 To 28th February 1918 (Volume 21)		
War Diary	U28e93 Ref Map Special Sh U1 To C6 Scale 1/10,000	01/02/1918	07/02/1918
War Diary	U.26c71 Ref Map Special St U1 to C6 Scale 1/10,000	07/02/1918	12/02/1918
War Diary	Belfast Camp Ervillers	12/02/1918	28/02/1918
Heading	40th Division. 121st Infantry Brigade. War Diary 13th Battalion The Yorkshire Regiment March 1918		
Heading	War Diary of 13th (Service) Battalion Yorkshire Regiment from March 1st 1918 to March 31st 1918 (Volume 22)		
War Diary	Bailleulval Ref Lens II Map	01/03/1918	11/03/1918
War Diary	Hendecourt	12/03/1918	20/03/1918
War Diary	St. Leger B.2.d.	21/03/1918	21/03/1918
War Diary	St Leger Sunken Rd B.4.b.	22/03/1918	22/03/1918
War Diary	Ervillers B.8.c.40.10	23/03/1918	25/03/1918

War Diary	Douchy-les-Ayette Ref Lens II	26/03/1918	26/03/1918
War Diary	Bienvillers	26/03/1918	26/03/1918
War Diary	Bailleulval	27/03/1918	27/03/1918
War Diary	Habarco	28/03/1918	28/03/1918
War Diary	Sus-St-Leger	29/03/1918	29/03/1918
War Diary	Marquay.	30/03/1918	30/03/1918
War Diary	Neuf Berquin.	31/03/1918	31/03/1918
Heading	40th Division. 121st Infantry Brigade. War Diary 13th Battalion Yorkshire Regiment. April 1918		
War Diary	Neuf Berquin	01/04/1918	01/04/1918
War Diary	Bois-Grenier	02/04/1918	09/04/1918
War Diary	Bois Grenier	09/04/1918	10/04/1918
War Diary	Touquet Parmentier	10/04/1918	11/04/1918
War Diary	Pont D'Achelles	11/04/1918	11/04/1918
War Diary	Strazeele	12/04/1918	13/04/1918
War Diary	St Martin-Au-Laeurt.	20/04/1918	21/04/1918
War Diary	Proven	28/04/1918	30/04/1918
Heading	25th Division 74th Infy Bde 13th Bn Yorkshire Regt Jly 1918 Serving in U.K. 40 Div. 121 Bde June 1916		
Heading	War Diary of 13th (Service) Battalion Yorkshire Regiments From 1st May 1918 To 31st May 1918 (Volume 24)		
War Diary	Proven	01/05/1918	01/05/1918
War Diary	Oudezeele	02/05/1918	02/05/1918
War Diary	Kinderbelck	03/05/1918	09/05/1918
War Diary	Oudeleele	10/05/1918	10/05/1918
War Diary	Kinderbelck	10/05/1918	10/05/1918
War Diary	Oudezeele	11/05/1918	31/05/1918
Miscellaneous	13th (Service) Bn. Yorkshire Regt. Appendix 'A' issued with War Diary for May 1918		
Heading	War Diary of 13th (Service) Battalion Yorkshire Regiment July 1st 1918 To July 31st 1918		
War Diary	Magtchett Carnk Farmbarough	01/07/1918	18/07/1918
War Diary	Aldeburgh Saiffock	20/07/1918	31/07/1918
War Diary	Aldeburgh Saiffock	19/07/1918	31/07/1918

WO 95/21992

40TH DIVISION
121ST INFY BDE

13TH BN YORKSHIRE REGT
JUN 1916 - JLY 1918

To UK

Original.

40 July
13 Yorks Ry
Vol 2

Confidential.

WAR DIARY

of

13th (S) Battalion Yorkshire Regiment.

From 1st July, 1916 to 31st July, 1916.

(Volume 2)

June
12/40
XL Vol 1

WAR DIARY or INTELLIGENCE SUMMARY

13th (SERVICE) Bn. YORKSHIRE REGT.

(Erase heading not required.)

Army Form C. 2118

Place	Date	Hour	Summary of Events and Information	Remarks and references to Appendices
Wath	27.5.16		The Battn. was ordered to mobilise on 27-5-16. Strength 33 officers & 991 other ranks. Mobilisation was completed this day. The invoice to the Bank and Vice to the KO in Sonneville on 28th May the 26th May the 13 officers complimenting 28 the steadiness of all ranks on parade.	
Withui	28.5.16		The Battn. under the command of Major G.E. Gibb (Lt. Col. [illegible]) entrained at Wateen Stn. in the centre the Strength being 34 officers and 995-978th ranks arriving at Southampton at 1am & Special trains at 6am and 3pm respectively. Embarkation was delayed owing to rough weather.	
Southampton	6		The Battn embarked at H.M. transports Caesarea, excellen[?] Torpedo boats acted as an [illegible] rough weather in Lowre was reached about 3am. The Battn was marched to Sequirilt.	
La Havre to [illegible]			Disembarkation took place at 7am & the Battn marched to La Vink[?] comp, about 4 miles, where the Battn entrained up on[?] arrive at 10 pm after 2 days sick the Battn entrained at La Havre at 12 mn.	

WAR DIARY
or
INTELLIGENCE SUMMARY
(Erase heading not required.)

Army Form C. 2118

13th (SERVICE) Bn. YORKSHIRE REGT.

Place	Date	Hour	Summary of Events and Information	Remarks and references to Appendices
Ham-en-Artois	7.1.16		A/C travelling to terms on the train the Batt. detrained at Lillers. The men travelled in fine trucks. There were till 31 men, but until ten men to 12 who travelled by ordinary trains, the men had breakfast on arriving at Lillers & then marched 2½ miles to Ham-en-Artois, coming billeted in farm buildings. The men were quite comfortable, fresh straw being provided, & were not overcrowded.	
Ham-en-Artois	8.1.16		The Batt. re-commenced training. Bombing grounds, rifle ranges for Lewis gun & snipers, also ranges for Rifle were available. Two coys marched to these ranges daily. The coys not detailed as such on duty, one spent in trench making (all ranging), even the following day.	
Ham-en-Artois	13.1.16		The B** with Batt of 69 & 81** Middlesex each Bn in the 121st Brigade were inspected by the Brigade Commander, Brigadier Sir Charles Turnard who completed the Cd. On the most rehearsal of the men, also there general steadiness on Parade. Business were served after the inspection, the Bn marched past in column of route.	

WAR DIARY or INTELLIGENCE SUMMARY

Army Form C. 2118

13th (SERVICE) Bn. YORKSHIRE REGT.

Place	Date	Hour	Summary of Events and Information	Remarks and references to Appendices
Mametz- en-Ruits	19.7.16		The Bn. lt moved from Ham-en-Artois to Mametz-en-Ruits by march route. Reveille 3am:- at 6 am arrived at Mametz-en-Ruits at 11.30 am. Settled in scan extruedthings & miners kitchens	
Mametz- les-Ruits	20.7.16		The Bn. continued training on areas being allotted by H.Q. 121st Inf. Bde., Ref. Map France, Sheet 23.6.16. P/12/D. On this ground training with Live Bombs, Wiring, Sniping, Rifles, Bayonet work & Trench work is carried out.	
Mametz- les-Ruits	21.7.16		The whole Regt. were able to turn in Baths discovered in Ecole Nor. 60 men at a time it took about 5 hours per man which served the 16th in our quite Another batch from Infantry & officers Baths were available. Were a great boon to the men.	
Mametz- les-Ruits	24.6.16		The Brigade being in Reserve The Bn was required to be held in readiness to move within five hours notice. The Bn was given the code name of Defence the Brigade code name being Marathon.	

WAR DIARY or INTELLIGENCE SUMMARY 13th (SERVICE) Bn. YORKSHIRE REGT.

Army Form C. 2118

(Erase heading not required.)

Instructions regarding War Diaries and Intelligence Summaries are contained in F.S. Regs., Part II. and the Staff Manual respectively. Title Pages will be prepared in manuscript.

Place	Date	Hour	Summary of Events and Information	Remarks and references to Appendices
Bruay	April 25th/16		WO. B.172 No 10 Green was selected as tunnelling in the 15th Brigade relieving 62nd (?) Infantry Brigade. This being the first draft since the Battalion arrived in France.	
Bruay	April 28th/16		The Bn. was ordered to Culonne for three Trench instructions. A & B being attached to 1st Cameron Highlanders & C & D Coys to 1st Cameron Highrs. Two platoons of each coy being in front line trenches & two platoons in support trenches. The trenches were occupied up to 6 ft. (Why pellen attached).	
Culonne	April 29th/16		Four casualties occurred. No 29165 Sergt W. Hensley A Coy, 27990 Pte P. Taylor, 23651 Pte L. Bully were killed by a Trench mortar. No 29615 Pte W. Eardle with his with a rifle as he was in trench & dugout. These men were buried in Culonne Cemetery between brigade work placed at their head.	
Culonne	April 30th/16		The training was carried on. The men & men seem to be in very cheerful this no casualty occurred. The men kept very cheerful took great interest in their first experience of trench warfare	

13th (Service) Battalion Yorkshire Regt.

NOMINAL ROLL OF OFFICERS WITH THE BATTALION.

Lieut. Colonel	Falls	H.E.
Major	Tristram	F.T.
"	Fox	W.
Captain	Ryan	T.
"	Bigg-Wither	H.G.
"	Smith	H.
"	Stewart	J.R.
"	Kirby	J.A.
"	Mansfield	J.A.
"	Hopkins	T.H.C.
Lieutenant	Vickers	N.M.
"	Elborne	C.C.
"	Harle	N.V.
"	Jones	A.A.H.
"	Jones	L.H.
"	Phillips	P.M.
"	Pickard	T.K.
"	Worthington	G.F.P.
2nd Lieutenant	Wallis	C.H.
"	Johns	J.F.
"	Hope	P.B.
"	Seager	H.B.
"	Simpkin	H.H.
"	Simpkin	A.W.
"	Millar	D.C.R.
"	Graves	H.J.
"	Kelly	M.W.J.
"	Bayles	J.H.G.
"	Walton	H.W.
"	Dowton	F.H.
"	Scott	W.
Captain	Virgo	J.
Lt. & Q.M.	Johnson	G.
Lt.	Brownlie	W. (R.A.M.C.)

WAR DIARY or INTELLIGENCE SUMMARY

Army Form C. 2118
13th (SERVICE) Bn. YORKSHIRE REGT.

Place	Date	Hour	Summary of Events and Information	Remarks and references to Appendices
Colonne	1/6		Tour still undergoing Trench training on the platoon basis. A Yst. Coy being attached to the Yorkshire Watch. & C & D Coy to the Yorkshire Regt. Nr 29867 Pte H Horton & 29753 Pte Lee Gibson both of A Coy were wounded & evacuated to the 141st Field Ambulance.	
Colonne	2/6		Shelling was heavy in this Sector & three men were hit by it early morning. There total 6 killed since arriving in the Trenches. They were No. 29466 Pte McTavish & No. 29487 Pte H Dunn & 29424 L. Cpl Funk were buried by a heavy trench mortar & another in trench 50 they were dug out during the night & buried at Colonne. Orders were received to have the Trenches returned to Maricourt-sur-Puits. Platoons left at 10 minutes intervals & formed up in groups on arriving at Ferfeuil, where the Battalion fitted into motor buses & were waiting with a hot dinner after dinner the Coys marched to their Billets in Bieu, arriving very tired but everyone had had seen their first experience of French warfare were very cheerful when leaving the Trenches. No 29818 Pte W Carlisle was accidentally shot. The total casualties during this training	

Army Form C. 2118

WAR DIARY
or
INTELLIGENCE SUMMARY
(Erase heading not required.)

13th (SERVICE) Bn. YORKSHIRE REGT.

Instructions regarding War Diaries and Intelligence Summaries are contained in F.S. Regs., Part II. and the Staff Manual respectively. Title Pages will be prepared in manuscript.

Place	Date	Hour	Summary of Events and Information	Remarks and references to Appendices
Colonne	2/7/16		was seven killed one accidentally killed & two wounded	
Maroil to Ruitz	3/7/16		Brigade orders were received at 5.30 am that the 121st Infy Rgt were to relieve the 2nd Infy Bde in the Maroc sector by the 1st Division. On orders were were going to move at 8 am D Coy leaving. Relations at 8.0 & to move at 8 am D Coy having not & Luncheon, the Coy proto the men marched very well. On arrival at Maroc, the Bn was placed in Reserve & received billets in N. Maroc villas holding H.Q. & 3 men. The accommodation provided. Rations were brought up from Les Brebis at night. In Maroc our artillery were stationed. The Guns being mostly in houses & were very carefully concealed. The enemy were continually shelling this place, apparently searching for the guns.	
Maroc	4/7/16		Orders were received to move into support to relieve the 21st Middlesex Regt who were to relieve the 12th Suffolk Regt. The latter being in the front line trenches. The Bn Headquarters & two Coys were in support billets adjacent to those in N. Maroc. A Coy occupying trenches in the old German Line. B Coy occupying Bullet Pt & Maroc.	

WAR DIARY
or
INTELLIGENCE SUMMARY

Army Form C. 2118

13th (SERVICE) Bn. YORKSHIRE REGT.

3

Place	Date	Hour	Summary of Events and Information	Remarks and references to Appendices
Maroc	6/7/16		A very perfect stillness in O.G.1. were continually being sniped. No 2/6th Sgt. H Bowry being hit in the leg by a sniper. We were evacuated to 137 Field Ambulance.	
Maroc	7/7/16		The Bn are still in support. Found working parties myself for the 2 two midnight Pty 800 & 300 men. More mix the Trench to be improved. The Trenches being in a very bad state. Cas. only N° 25546 Pte A Renwick D Coy. was wounded out of the whole of these working parties.	
Maroc	8/7/16		On this date there was only one casualty N° 24715 Pte J Huggon C Coy being badly wounded a Trench Mortar Bn when was attached to the 14th 18th Trench Mortar Battery.	
Maroc	10/7/16		Orders were received that the 121st Infy Bde would be relieved by the — 120th Infy Bde in the Maroc Section on the 11th/7 & 12th/7 July. No Casualties occurred on this date.	

WAR DIARY or INTELLIGENCE SUMMARY

Army Form C. 2118

13th (SERVICE) Bn. YORKSHIRE REGT.

Place	Date	Hour	Summary of Events and Information	Remarks and references to Appendices
Zea-Vouba	11/7/16		The Bn. was relieved by the 11th Bn Argyll & Sutherland Regt. on the night which day we took over the Billets occupied by that Bn. in Zea-Vouba.	
— do —	12/7/16		The Bn. rested on this date, cleaning up only being done.	
— do —	13.7.16		Training was continued on this day, allotted new Zea-breads where bomb throwing could also be practiced.	
— do —	16.7.16		The Bn. went to Bains-the-Frouvent for training in trench fighting during Trench improvements & Bomb Throwing returning at 6 pm on this date. Rifles were received that 18th Infy. Bde. would receive the 13.0.R. July 16th only & most relief having to be completed at 8 pm by 18th July. At 10 pm on 15th & 16 inst. This Batn. to whom were allotted to the Batt. no. 15th & 16 inst. This Batn. were under firing line arrangements. 40 men every 20 minutes could be bathed. At these Baths no every man handed in his dirty underclothing & received clean in exchange. The Bath & change of clothing was much appreciated by the men.	

WAR DIARY or INTELLIGENCE SUMMARY

13th (SERVICE) Bn. YORKSHIRE REGT.

Army Form C. 2118

Place	Date	Hour	Summary of Events and Information	Remarks and references to Appendices
MARUE	17.7.16		On this date the Bttn. the Front Line from the Border Barriers to Munster. This was in Front Line & this coys in support line. The Trenches were found in a very bad condition having been heavily shelled by the enemy. The Bn received orders to relieve units in the line without casualties. It be done. They received orders complete at 6 Pm without casualties. The unit on the right of this Bn (Munster) section was the 120th Infy Bde occupying the Chinese section & on the left in Brigade support, the 6th Middlesex occupied the left sub section of the Calonne section	
MARUE	18.7.16		There were 4 wounded on this date, three of whom were at the Corps Rest Station	
— do —	19.7.16		No. 24196 L/Cpl Statton, Appleton & Pte 1429674 Pte Brewer were killed, both of D Coy H.E. Shells being the cause	
— do —	20.7.16		No. 23147 L/C Blackburn of C Coy was killed by Shrapnel & No. 29405 Pte Turner E.A. A. was wounded & died in 33rd C.C.S.	

WAR DIARY or INTELLIGENCE SUMMARY

Army Form C. 2118

13th (SERVICE) Bn. YORKSHIRE REGT.

6

Place	Date	Hour	Summary of Events and Information	Remarks and references to Appendices
Maroc	20/6		On this date the enemy & the casualty being 28946/2 L/C. W. Wetherup to 8. Day.	
-11-	21/6		On this the enemy were very quiet only two men being reported as slightly wounded	
-11-	22/6		On this date the toys changed over & also my company up the front line position of C & B coy the latter completely the positions being held by the former. Only one casualty occurred on this date No. 29564 P. Philips A/S Coy being wounded	
-11-	24/6		No. 29467 Madams G. Arey was killed on this date this man was being wounded	
-11-	24/6		2/Lt J.G. White was evacuated to the C.C.S. suffering debility & 2/Lt H. Simpkin was admitted to Hosp — do — influenza	

Army Form C. 2118

WAR DIARY
or
INTELLIGENCE SUMMARY
(Erase heading not required.)

13th (SERVICE) Bn. YORKSHIRE REGT.

Place	Date	Hour	Summary of Events and Information	Remarks and references to Appendices
25th to wave	25th		Lt Col A.B. Gallo Connolly was admitted to hosp. & evacuated to the C.C.S. on this date & the command devolved on the 15th devolved on Major L.T. Burnham.	
—"—	26th		There was very little was wounded on this day by shrapnel. The enemy shewing very quiet	
—"—	27th		On this day the enemy were very active. 2/Lt 25789 2nd Lt Relek Perry killed & others less wounded. 2/Lieut N.J. Abbot, R. Longley & L.A. Mumbs were posted from 14 Reserve B[?] The command of the Bn was reassumed provisionally on this date by Major R.W. Parker who was 2nd in command of the 2nd/8th Middlesex Regt. Vice Lt Col A.B. Gallo evacuated	
—"—	28th		On this date the Sutton trench was held by the Bn being 2nd & 1st Sub section. The arena (experiment) to "women etcphmone" which ran from the trunk (experiment) to "women etcphmone" from 12 yards R of I (?) were attached to assist in holding the entire trench. Those were only two worked as on this date	

Army Form C. 2118

WAR DIARY
or
INTELLIGENCE SUMMARY
(Erase heading not required.)

13th (SERVICE) Bn. YORKSHIRE REGT.

Instructions regarding War Diaries and Intelligence Summaries are contained in F. S. Regs., Part II. and the Staff Manual respectively. Title Pages will be prepared in manuscript.

Place	Date	Hour	Summary of Events and Information	Remarks and references to Appendices
Mercatel No 1 Sub Section Left	29.7.16		The double crater which had been held by 2nd/Suffolks & 8th KRRC was reached & 60 O.Ranks was relieved by one officer & 35 O.Ranks of the Bn. & 1 Officer & 25 Other ranks of the 12th Works Bn. Only one casualty received on this date, this being a wounded case	
— " —				
— " —	30.7.16		A & B Coys relieved C & D Coys from the front line trenches. This relief was completed by 7 a.m. There were no casualties on this date. The horse-lines [being?] very quiet. No 29554 Pte Porter T who was admitted to 34th F.A. on this date died the same day at the 33rd C.C.S.	
— " —	31.7.16		There was only one casualty on this date. No 29685 Pte Plant being hit with shrapnel	

In the Field
1st August, 1916.

B. Baker Major
Commandg 13th (S). Bn. Yorks. Regt.

Army Form C. 2118

WAR DIARY

13th (SERVICE) Bn. YORKSHIRE REGT.

INTELLIGENCE SUMMARY

(Erase heading not required.)

Vol 3

Confidential

War Diary
of
13th (Service) Battalion, Yorkshire Regiment.

From 1st August, 1916. To 31st August, 1916.
(Volume 3).

WAR DIARY or INTELLIGENCE SUMMARY

Army Form C. 2118

13th (SERVICE) Bn. YORKSHIRE REGT.

Place	Date	Hour	Summary of Events and Information	Remarks and references to Appendices
MAROC	1-8-16		The Bn was still in the Front Line Trenches on this date, only one casualty occurred N.29.d.5 Pte W. Harper being hit with a rifle grenade. (A coy)	
-do-	2-8-16		Two casualties occurred on this date from Rifle Grenades N.29.6.2.5 Sgt F. Robinson (B coy) & N.29.8.4.3 Pte E. Carlin (C coy). This N.C.O. & man were of the party building the DOUBLE CRASSIER	
-do-	3-8-16		On this date Lieut N.M. Vickers was in charge of a patrol reconnoitering the crater. He received the enemy's recognition sign & few bombs at the first one of which were thrown. He killed this officer. The patrol were not unfortunately hit from the enemy who entrenched & did not miss fire from the trench when the patrol retired. The officer until arriving there, gave no sign of being hit & when to Lieut T.K. Pyle hard who atone time without his assistance had a difficult & somewhat precarious recovery of brought in the body of Lieut Vickers. This he had alone, a difficult & somewhat precarious recovery on account of the bombs which were being thrown by the enemy. N.29.a.7.8. A.W.W. Coy. He was wounded by shrapnel N.30.a.4.8.6.7	

WAR DIARY
or
INTELLIGENCE SUMMARY

Army Form C. 2118
13th (SERVICE) Bn. YORKSHIRE REGT.

Place	Date	Hour	Summary of Events and Information	Remarks and references to Appendices
MAROC	3.8.16		Capt. T. Radcliffe D.S.O. was wounded by rifle grenade also on this date. An incident or two were received that this rifle would be relieved on the 4th by the 12.D.L.I.	
–do–	4.8.16		The Bn was relieved from the front line by the 11th Kings Own Yorks Lancaster Regt & returned to rest billets in Les Brebis or occupying the billets previously occupied by the Bn on arriving at Les Brebis. The O.C. discovered a place where infantry could be conveniently carried out to the great satisfaction of all ranks who had been in the front line for 18 days total. The 13th Bn had been in the front line for 18 days. Total casualties being for this period 10 officers & other ranks killed & 29 other ranks wounded & 2 shell shock cases due to enemy shell fire.	
Les Brebis	5.8.16		This being the first day out of the trenches the Bn was allowed to rest	
–do–	6.8.16		The Divisional Baths were allotted to the Bn on this date when all ranks were were allowed a hot bath & a change of	

WAR DIARY or INTELLIGENCE SUMMARY

13th (SERVICE) Bn. YORKSHIRE REGT.

Army Form C. 2118

(3)

Place	Date	Hour	Summary of Events and Information	Remarks and references to Appendices
Les Boves	6.8.16 & 8.8.16		of underclothing. The men hand in their dirty linen & receive clean in exchange.	
— do —	7.8.16		The Bn was allotted a training ground in the district. Bois-du-Warnimont where training was carried out at night. An outpost scheme was carried out the Bn returning to billets in the early hours of the following day.	
— do —	8.8.16		This date was devoted to training under Bn arrangements in wiring, physical training, drill, bombing, practice range practice for selected shots etc.	
— do —	9.8.16		Lieut C.C. Elborne was appointed Bn Intelligence Officer in relief of Brev. Lt. Morris who is attached to the 2/5 Bn. Middlesex Regt. The Bn. continued training as for the 8/6.	
— do —	10.8.16		Orders were received that the 121st Infy Bde. would relieve the 120th Infy Bde. in the Maroc Section on the 12th August. The Bn. continued training as on the previous day.	

WAR DIARY
INTELLIGENCE SUMMARY
13th (SERVICE) Bn. YORKSHIRE REGT.

Army Form C. 2118

(4)

Place	Date	Hour	Summary of Events and Information	Remarks and references to Appendices
LES BREBIS	11.8.16		The Bn continued training under Coy arrangements. Great use being made of the trenches at the Les Brebis Mine (Posse No 6 de Bethune)	
MAROC	12.8.16		The Bn relieved the 14th Bn Argyle & Sutherland Highlanders in Rly Support on this date. A Company occupying O.4.1 B, C, & D Coys in billets in MAROC. The relief being completed by 9 pm	
— do —	15.8.16		There was one casualty on this date No 29535 Pte Dawson B Coy of the 1st Line Transport who was stationed in Les Brebis where heavy shelling had occurred a number of inhabitants being injured. This man was admitted to hospital suffering shell shock. On this date No. 6 Stationary orders were received by which the name of Lieut. T.K. Pickard appeared as having been awarded the Military Cross by the F.O.C. in chief for the following act of gallantry — On the night of the 3/4 of August 1916 a patrol of one officer & two men went out to reconnoitre a German Sap. Lieut T.K. Pickard on hearing that the patrol had been fired on by the enemy & that only two men had returned	

WAR DIARY
INTELLIGENCE SUMMARY

Army Form C. 2118

13th (SERVICE) Bn. YORKSHIRE REGT.

(5)

Instructions regarding War Diaries and Intelligence Summaries are contained in F.S. Regs., Part II. and the Staff Manual respectively. Title Pages will be prepared in manuscript.

Place	Date	Hour	Summary of Events and Information	Remarks and references to Appendices
MAPLE	15.8.16		Volunteered to search for the officer & bring him in. This he did alone, removing the officer out of the German wire, a difficult & dangerous operation on account of the bombs that were being thrown by the enemy. Unhappily the officer was found to be dead when brought in. 2nd Lieut Pickard. This was the first Military Cross to be awarded in this Division and honor of which the Bn is proud to claim.	
-do-	16.8.16		On this date the billets round the support Bn head-quarters were shelled by the enemy, the enemy 3 casualties in the Bn. W.O. 23636 L/Cpl E Reynolds being killed & W.O. 29670 Pte E Chambers W. 24793 Pte E. Kilburn being wounded. These men were all signallers were out repairing the telephone lines which had previously been cut by a shell. L/Cpl Reynolds was a very efficient Sig-naller.	

WAR DIARY
INTELLIGENCE SUMMARY
(Erase heading not required.)

Army Form C. 2118

13th (SERVICE) Bn. YORKSHIRE REGT.

Place	Date	Hour	Summary of Events and Information	Remarks and references to Appendices
MARCH	18 16		No 9628 Pte A Sewbrook was wounded on this date by a sniper whilst in O.P.1. Orders were received on this date for the Bn to occupy the MARCH LEFT Sub section the relieving the 21st Bn Middlesex Regt on the 20/3/16. Our Bombers will those of the 20th Middlesex Regt holding the DOUVE CRASSIER	
-do-	19 3/16		Machine gunners relieved those of the 21st Middlesex Regt on this date the relief being completed by 4 pm.	
-do-	20 3/16	8	The Bn relieved the 21st Bn Middlesex Regt in the MARCH LEFT Sub-Section on this date. The relief was completed by 6.30 am. D Coy occupied the front line trenches from the DOUVE CRASSIER to the CRATERS exclusive of, from the CRATERS exclusive to HAYMARKET. B Coy being in support B Coy & A Coy in support to do so. There were no casualties on this date.	
-do-	21 16		No 29393 Coy Sgt Major Shirley of D Coy was killed by a sniper this Coy. is an excellent N.O. & will be greatly missed by his Coy. No 24922 Pte Lundsheart of the	

WAR DIARY or INTELLIGENCE SUMMARY

Army Form C. 2118

13th (SERVICE) Bn. YORKSHIRE REGT.

Place	Date	Hour	Summary of Events and Information	Remarks and references to Appendices
MAROC	21/6		Same tour but from wounds received at the same time as Private No.23690 P.W. Hargrove of B. Coy were wounded by shrapnel S.M. Shelby of W.Wilson & Walters were injured in MAROC.	
–do–	22/6		No.29842 Pte. T.W.H. Redburn was killed by Trench Mortar & was buried in MAROC. No.25758 Pte. C. Major Pte. D.29741 Pte. Langley T.H. Coy No.29694 Pte. L. Pickering C were all wounded by Trench Mortar on this date.	
–do–	23/6		On this date No.29691 Pte A. Fittill of B. Coy was killed by rifle grenade was buried in MAROC a month extract N.E.R.	
–do–	24/6		On this date B Coy relieved D in the front line 6 Coy relieving C. A Coy & C taking over the Trenches previously occupied by the A & B Coy. The NORTH-N STAFFS was also relieved by front line into 10 numbers of Lieut H.J. Graves being in command. The S. WYKEHAM BRASSIER was killed by the 2nd MIDDLESEX Bombers. Both Co.A.S.I. 1278 were under the Command of O.C. MAROC LEFT SUB SECTION. (MAJOR B.G. Baker).	

WAR DIARY

Army Form C. 2118

INTELLIGENCE SUMMARY 13th (SERVICE) Bn. YORKSHIRE REGT.

(Erase heading not required.)

Place	Date	Hour	Summary of Events and Information	Remarks and references to Appendices
MAROC	24/6		There was only one casualty from this date No 23101 Pte B Wing of A Coy being wounded by a rifle grenade	
—do—	25/6		Major R.J. Baker assumed the Temporary Rank of Lt. Col on this date. 2nd Lieut W.N. Ford joined the Bn. he being transferred from 3rd W. Yorks Regt & to act under 2/O for experience for 3 days. Pte Nos 29783 Lee Cpl Denniss & Pte No 29483 P.A. Dredge were both killed by a trench mortar shell & No. 30455 C. Crassir & No 28749 Hooton Pte A Coy was wounded at the place.	
—do—	26/6		There was only one casualty on this date No 23574 Pte A. Minto B/Coy being wounded by a rifle grenade	
—do—	27/6		Orders were received from H.Q. 121st Infy Bde that the Bn. would be relieved on 28 & 29th inst by 9/Norfolk Regt & that the Bn. would move into support in LE WARRE. On this night a such [?] was arranged for in the area of the Ypres by the TRIANGLE. Canadian Torpedoes were used for cutting the wire. The raiding parties consist in	

WAR DIARY
INTELLIGENCE SUMMARY
(Erase heading not required.)

13th (SERVICE) Bn. YORKSHIRE REGT.

Army Form C. 2118

Place	Date	Hour	Summary of Events and Information	Remarks and references to Appendices
MAFO	27/9/16		no-man's land ready to rush the gap if found sufficiently cut. The Torpedoes were exploded by electricity from the front line trenches. Scouts were then sent forward to inspect & were where the wire was with them to ascertain whether a sufficient gap had been made to enable the raiders to get through. Unfortunately this found that the wire was insufficiently cut by the explosion. The raiders were withdrawn without casualty. The men worked very well, especially the men under Cpl. N.Y. Kirkpatrick who went out, but to the superior in position returned in 3/4 of an hour. All ranks were disappointed on having to withdraw without any fighting taken place. The details of the raid were drawn up by Lt Col. B.J. Parks Capt A.G. Beggs-Withers of the R.1922. See from party & Capt A. Smith of the LEFT section party.	answer Report attached
-/-	28/9		The 10th was relieved by the 21st Bn. Middlesex Regt on this date. The relief being completed by 9 am.	

WAR DIARY or INTELLIGENCE SUMMARY

Army Form C. 2118

13th (SERVICE) Bn. YORKSHIRE REGT.

Place	Date	Hour	Summary of Events and Information	Remarks and references to Appendices
MARCOL	28/6		Occupied Billets in N.F. MAROC as Bn in support. A Coy who had previously occupied D.H.Q when Bn in support were put into billets. The Divisional Baths were allotted to the Bn from 1pm return all ranks were enabled to obtain a change of underclothing. Lt. Platoon of C Coy took over Traverse Keep in this new arrangement this Keep is held by the Bn.	
—Do—	29/6		On this date Lieut C.F. Jemmison 92nd I.M.G. working which the Bn, on being re-enforced from the 57th Infantry Base Depot with three officers (two other & Nine other Ranks joined the 115th Reserve Bn when they & Joined the 115th Reserve Bn when they were ordered.	
—Do—	30/6		2/Lieut A.Y. ABBOTT who went to Ph 12th when proceeding in this officer previously served in the 14th Reserve Bn which is also a profits Bn. Given opinions to serve with a unit with which he considered he could do more useful work, having been a Corporal before receiving a commission	

WAR DIARY
INTELLIGENCE SUMMARY
(Erase heading not required.)

Army Form C. 2118

13th (SERVICE) Bn. YORKSHIRE REGT.

Place	Date	Hour	Summary of Events and Information	Remarks and references to Appendices
MAROC	31/8/16		Orders were received on this date to relieve the 12th Bn. Loyal N. Lancashire Regt. in the MAROC LEFT SUB Section on 1-8-16. The Bn. will thus occupy the front line after being in support for 4 days.	

31-8-16

J F Baber
Lt Col
Commdg 13th Bn Yorks Regt

Army Form C. 2118

WAR DIARY
or
INTELLIGENCE SUMMARY   13th (SERVICE) Bn. YORKSHIRE REGT.   Vol 4
(Erase heading not required.)

Summary of Events and Information

CONFIDENTIAL.

WAR DIARY

OF

13th (Service) Battalion Yorkshire Regiment

From 1st September 1916 To. 31st September 1916.

(VOLUME 4.)

WAR DIARY
INTELLIGENCE SUMMARY

Army Form C.,2118

13th (SERVICE) Bn. YORKSHIRE REGT.

Place	Date	Hour	Summary of Events and Information	Remarks and references to Appendices
MAROC	1-9-16		The Bn relieved the 21st Middlesex Regt in trenches LEE Sub SECTION on this date, relief being by 4 am.	
-DO-	2-9-16		On this date LP 24/762 Pte S. Harris was killed by a sniper & 29865 Lee Corporal A. Deery & W.21647 L. Corporal Boyd both by rifle grenades on DOUBLE CRASSIER	
-DO-	3-9-16	W.O.93110 Pte J M Crumbly	A coy was relieved by 2nd Welch. Orders were received that 12nd July tube would be seiged in M R de SECTION by 12.00 midnight Relieve out 12.5 Sept	
-DO-	4-9-16		Enemy were very quiet on this date. No casualties occurring the weather has been very showery & some trenches had gotten wet & all the time during this there was no taking up or relieving them	
-DO-	5-9-16		The Bn was relieved by the 14th Argyll & Sutherland Highlanders on this date relief being completed by 1pm. The Bn took up billets at MISH FLAYS own through Loires its Regt in LES BREBIS	

WAR DIARY
or
INTELLIGENCE SUMMARY

(Erase heading not required.)

Army Form C. 2118

2 / 13th (SERVICE) Bn. YORKSHIRE REGT.

Place	Date	Hour	Summary of Events and Information	Remarks and references to Appendices
LES 10 RE 16/5	6.9.16		The Men were bathed at the Mine in LES 10 RE 218 where the men boiled swim. Clothing was refused & new clothing issued & all were ordered to have a thorough clean up. In the evening more than half the Bn. had to be on fatigue	
—"—	7/9/16		Training was continued. Bombing grounds, Rifle Range Musing grounds, being visited to coys. but different times during the day	
—"—	8/9/16		The whole Bn. went to the training ground at POIS-du-FROISSART where Coys. unfilled section & coy commanders was carried out In the afternoon an attack was carried out. The weather was very fine & the men thoroughly enjoyed the change from the trenches	
—"—	9/9/16		Order were received that the 18th Infy. Bde. would relieve the 119th Bde in the POS. SECTION on 11th & 12th Sept. relief to be completed by 6 am 12th SEPT	

Army Form C. 2118

WAR DIARY
INTELLIGENCE SUMMARY
(Erase heading not required.)

3.

13th (SERVICE) Bn. YORKSHIRE REGT.

Place	Date	Hour	Summary of Events and Information	Remarks and references to Appendices
PREVETTE PASSAGE LOOS	13/9/16		The Bn relieved 12th S.W.B. in LOOS SUBSECT. SECTOR A & C Coys occupying Bullets in the EN CLOSURE. B Coy & Platoon MAQUE LINE & Platoons LENS ROAD REDOUBT. D Coy DUKE ST. The relief was completed by 3 p.m.	
— do —	14/9/16		The Bn were employed on fatigues during the 4 days they were in Support. This typ of all men during any job of the employed men for their work for this date will be given for the Bn to relieve the 20 Middlesex in Brigade Reserve in MAROC.	
MAROC	15/9/16		The Bn moved in – to Brigade Reserve in MAROC relief being completed by 7 p.m. These billets were very good & much improved	
— " —	16/9/16		The Bn was employed to do a certain amount of Training whilst in Reserve. Parade under coy arrangements in no. till from 5 p.m. to 7 p.m. Items were found in which relieves could be given there being also a practice ground where Bombs could be thrown & also revolver practice could be carried. There were very few fatigues found	

WAR DIARY of INTELLIGENCE SUMMARY

Army Form C. 2118

13th (SERVICE) Bn. YORKSHIRE REGT.

Place	Date	Hour	Summary of Events and Information	Remarks and references to Appendices
MAROC	16/9/16		& the men were ordered to have a good rest here	
-Do-	17/9/16		Orders were received on this date to relieve the 21st Middlesex Regt in the Right Sub Section LOOS. No.29775 Pte a Webster "B" Coy attached 18th Trench Mortar Battery was wounded by an aerial dart.	
LOOS	18/9/16		The Bn. relieved the 21st MIDDX ESEX REGT in the LOOS Right Sub SECTION. "C" Coy occupying the Front Line from BOYAU 31 to 86 inclusive. A Coy 86 exclusive to 39 inclusive VALLEY 9 ub SECTION being occupied by the Battalion Scot. Regt. C & D Coys occupied billets in the enclosure	
-Do-	20/9/16		No Casualties occurred in this enemy being very quiet in spite of our shelling with his front line coup Poachers & annoyed the enemy with rifle fire & Rifle grenades but his retaliation was very feeble	
-Do-	21/9/16		No.29613 Pte D Shire & No.23800 Pte W Asquith both "A" Coy died of wounds received from rifle grenades & were buried at	

Army Form. C. 2118

5.

WAR DIARY
or
INTELLIGENCE SUMMARY

13th (SERVICE) Bn. YORKSHIRE REGT.

(Erase heading not required.)

Instructions regarding War Diaries and Intelligence Summaries are contained in F. S. Regs., Part II. and the Staff Manual respectively. Title Pages will be prepared in manuscript.

Place	Date	Hour	Summary of Events and Information	Remarks and references to Appendices
LOOS	21/9/16		Phillips the three casualties in this section.	
-do-			No. 23162 Pte R. E. Ramsey & 20486 Pte S. Wilson were wounded by rifle grenade, while also 23978 Pte F. Nelson was also wounded.	
-do-	22/9/16		No. 28607 Pte H. Batty A/my died from rifle grenade wounds. 29644 Pte W. Barker & 24736 Pte R. Rush were wounded by rifle grenade. No. 29569 Pte A. Shaw B Coy was also wounded by shrapnel.	
-Do-	23/9/16		On this date a minor operation was carried by A & D Coy Bangalore Torpedoes being used to blow up the enemy wire, this was carried out successfully without any casualties. D & Coys relieved A & B Coys in the front line on this date.	
-Do-	24/9/16		On the night of the 24/25th an attempt was made by A Coy to enter the enemy trench through gaps made the	

WAR DIARY
INTELLIGENCE SUMMARY

Army Form C. 2118
13th (SERVICE) Bn. YORKSHIRE REGT.

Place	Date	Hour	Summary of Events and Information	Remarks and references to Appendices
LOOS	24/9/16		previous night. This was not successful but was found that the only trench mortars firing to us was seen up by Fry Street Mortars tenn line. On this night during wet weather) 10 Casualties & of whom were 5 to return to duty. During this night Lieut. F.M. Phillips who was found dead in the trench killed by rifle grenade. He was buried in PHILOSOPHE CEMErery. This officer was a very keen & fearless & was a very excellent officer.	
-Do-	23/9/16		2/Lt H Graves was wounded by shrapnel on this date. Another excellent officer, he did splendid work when their held the DOUBLE CRASSIER in MAROC. 04480 M.Sgt. R Mason 8 Yorks Regt was informed of Lieut & found on this date.	
-Do-	24/9/16		On this date another operation was carried out by 6 men under 2/Lt Langley. These was blown in by trifle charges near the LOOS CRASSIER all of which the enemy trench was quiet. The party were met with rockets bombs	

Army Form C. 2118

WAR DIARY
or
INTELLIGENCE SUMMARY
(Erase heading not required.)

13th (SERVICE) Bn. YORKSHIRE REGT.

Place	Date	Hour	Summary of Events and Information	Remarks and references to Appendices
LOOS	26/9/16		4 men being wounded. Lt Langley jumped into enemy trench but was hit by a bomb (Sgt Mucklewaite also jumped into the trench & found Lt Langley wounded). Pte 68 fired twice at Langley with his revolver, but was unable to do so. He managed to get out of the trench & Party had to retire owing to hostile bombing. Lt Langley being left in the hands of the enemy. This was most unfortunate as he was a promising young officer & was likely to do well.	
-Do-	27/9/16		In the a.m. the Bn. was relieved by the 21st Middlesex Regt. relief being completed by 9 a.m. The Bn. marched into Brilliant Headquarters being at BREVILLE PASSAGE in VILLAGE LINE. A Coy VILLAGE LINE & ENGROAD REDOUBT. B & C.B. Englebelmer. D Coy. D.H.R. S/Lieut W.V. Hodgson & L/B Phillips joined the Bn. on this date from 37th Infy Base DEPOT.	
-Do-	28/9/16		1767 L/Cpl Baker proceeded on leave to England. The command of the Bn. on devolving on Capt T. Ryan.	

1875   Wt. W.593/826 1,000,000 4/15 J.B.C. & A.   A.D.S.S./Forms/C. 2118.

WAR DIARY
or
INTELLIGENCE SUMMARY

Army Form C. 2118

13th (SERVICE) Bn. YORKSHIRE REGT.

Place	Date	Hour	Summary of Events and Information	Remarks and references to Appendices
TRENCHES PASSAGE 2005	30/9/14		Orders were received that the Bn would be relieved by the 20th Bn Middlesex Regt on 1/10/16. The Bn moving to MAROC in Brigade Reserve.	

Kings Copy Ragit.
to Lieut: Colonel
Comndg. 13th (S) Bn Yorkshire Regt.

WAR DIARY
INTELLIGENCE SUMMARY

Army Form C. 2118

13th (SERVICE) Bn. YORKSHIRE REGT.

Place	Date	Hour	Summary of Events and Information	Remarks and references to Appendices
TRENZE PASSAGE L.05	30/9/16		Orders were received that the Bn would be relieved by the 20th Middlesex Regt on 1/10/16. The Bn moving to MAROC in Brigade Reserve.	

Wm Baptaylk.
Lieut. Colonel.
Commdg 13th (S) Bn. Yorkshire Regt.

WAR DIARY
or
INTELLIGENCE SUMMARY.

13th (SERVICE) Bn. YORKSHIRE REGT.

Army Form C. 2118.

CONFIDENTIAL.

WAR DIARY

of

13th (Service) Battalion Yorkshire Regiment.

From 1st October 1916 To 31st October 1916.

(VOLUME 5).

Army Form C. 2118.

WAR DIARY 13th (SERVICE) Bn. YORKSHIRE REGT.

INTELLIGENCE SUMMARY.

(Erase heading not required.)

Instructions regarding War Diaries and Intelligence Summaries are contained in F. S. Regs., Part II and the Staff Manual respectively. Title pages will be prepared in manuscript.

Place	Date	Hour	Summary of Events and Information	Remarks and references to Appendices
MAROC	1-10-16		The Batt moved to MAROC on this date & occupied billets. The men were given baths, clothes & boots being repaired, & general cleaning took place which was very much needed after being in the Trenches	
-DO-	2-10-16		A certain amount of training was carried out in the buildings during the day in the early morning before it became light, the coys were able to drill by platoons	
-DO-	3-10-16		On this date orders were received that the Batt would relieve the 2/1st Middlesex Regt. in the LOOS Right Sub Sector	
LOOS	4-10-16		The Bn moved into to the LOOS Right Sub Section "B" Coy taking the line from Boyau 31 to MANING'S MOUND exclusive. "A" Coy MANING'S MOUND inclusive to Boyau 89. "C" Coys in HARPS craters being in "B" Coys area. The relief was completed by 4 p.m.	

Army Form C. 2118.

WAR DIARY

INTELLIGENCE SUMMARY. 13th (SERVICE) Bn. YORKSHIRE REGT.

(Erase heading not required.)

Instructions regarding War Diaries and Intelligence Summaries are contained in F. S. Regs., Part II. and the Staff Manual respectively. Title pages will be prepared in manuscript.

2.

Place	Date	Hour	Summary of Events and Information	Remarks and references to Appendices
100 S	5/10/16		There were four casualties on this all of "B" Coy. Three men were holding DEAD MANS Gap and were wounded by Trench Mortar.	
- DO -	6.10.16		There were 10 casualties on this date 7 by Trench Mortar, one of whom has since died. This made Sgt Haworth had been recommended for a commission. The remaining casualties were by Shrapnel & rifle fire. 2nd Lieut Mynd Kelly was also hit by Trench Mortar, his left arm having to be amputated. This was a very popular officer & is a great loss to the Bn.	
- DO -	7/10/16		On this date Cpl Henderson a very good sniping Cpl was wounded. This N.C.O. was continually doing good work & was noted for his excellent shooting ability on this night "B" Coy blew four gaps in the enemy wire	

WAR DIARY
or
INTELLIGENCE SUMMARY. 13th (SERVICE) Bn. YORKSHIRE REGT.

Army Form C. 2118.

3.

Place	Date	Hour	Summary of Events and Information	Remarks and references to Appendices
LOOS	7-10-16		round this long sap, 2nd Lieut Simpkin A.A.H. & 2nd Lieut Venables being in charge of separate parties. They did this work very quickly & well without a casualty. Capt Ryan in command of the Bn. had instructed them to enter the enemy's trenches if the blowing of the wire was successful. This they did, capturing two prisoners, & killing five others. There were other casualties amongst the enemy from our bombing party. This was a most successful raid & messages of congratulation were received from the Corps Commander, also from the Divisional & Brigade Commanders. We suffered no casualties.	
LOOS	8-10-16		Another raid took place on this night to "C" Coy entering the enemy's trenches & remaining there for 58 minutes. Numerous identifications were obtained but no prisoners were taken about 20 of the enemy were killed over	

Army Form. C. 2118.

WAR DIARY
or
INTELLIGENCE SUMMARY.
(Erase heading not required.)

13th (SERVICE) Bn. YORKSHIRE REGT.

4

Place	Date	Hour	Summary of Events and Information	Remarks and references to Appendices
OOS	8.10.16		Casualties being one officer & seven men being wounded one man single died(?). Lieut Hodgson & Lieut Perkins were in charge of the raiding parties, Capt. A Mansfield being in command of the Supports. 2/Lt Hodgson was hit in the knee on entering the Trenches but courageously kept on was the first to have the Trenches. Rifles Bayonets Gas Helmets, Identity discs & however straps, Steel Helmets papers & other articles found on dead Germans were brought back from by the raiders. That this raid? have been the most successful up to the present in the divisional area.	
OOS	9.10.16		N°30017 Pte W Rayns C Coy was killed by a Sniper on this date & was buried at Philosophe there were also 3 men wounded	
OOS	10.10.16		There was only one casualty on this date N°. 29723 Pte D.C.Guthrie	

2353 Wt. W2544/1454 700,000 5/15 D.D.&L. A.D.S.S./Forms/C. 2118.

Army Form C. 2118.

WAR DIARY
or
INTELLIGENCE SUMMARY.
(Erase heading not required.)

12th (SERVICE) Bn. YORKSHIRE REGT.

5.

Place	Date	Hour	Summary of Events and Information	Remarks and references to Appendices
LOOS	10.10.16		D Coy being wounded by Trench Mortar. The enemy's activity was very little since the raids.	
LOOS	11.10.16		The enemy's activity was very noticeable. The raids had evidently quietened him. There were no casualties. Orders were received that the 121st R.M.C. would relieve the 120th Bde in 14 Div Sector. The Bn being relieved by the 19th Royal Welsh Fusiliers.	
LOOS	12.10.16		On this date the Bn was relieved by the 19th Royal Welsh Fusiliers in the LOOS Section & moved into support Vb.coy occupying GUN TRENCH A coy LENS ROAD REDOUBT & Previse PASSAGE, C Coy 65 METRE REDOUBT & D coy NORTH nh REDOUBT. Relief being completed by 12 NOON. No 24694 Pte G.W. Ambler was killed by a Sniper & 21.29863 Pte B Thompson being wounded by a Trench Mortar	

WAR DIARY or INTELLIGENCE SUMMARY

Army Form C. 2118.

13th (SERVICE) Bn. YORKSHIRE REGT.

Place	Date	Hour	Summary of Events and Information	Remarks and references to Appendices
MAZING-ARBE	13.10.16		A & B Coy were relieved by the 20th Middlesex Regt & these Coys with Bn Headquarters moved to MAZINGARBE & received 2 coys of 12th Suffolk Regt sharing the reserve area of the Brigade with the 20th Middlesex Regt. In this place Huts are provided for the men & they are also enabled to bathe & clean up which they badly needed after their long spell in the trenches	
—Do—	14.10.16		A & B Coy continued training in musketry Rifle exercises etc. A 2nd suit of Service dress clothing was fitted. This is quite a new Regulation & enables the men to have a change of clothing	
—Do—	28.10.16		Orders were received on this date that the Bn would be relieved in MAZINGARBE by the 21st Middlesex Regt & proceed to 141 BIS SECTION and occupy the LEFT SUB SECTOR.	

Army Form C. 2118.

WAR DIARY
or
INTELLIGENCE SUMMARY.
(Erase heading not required.)

13th (SERVICE) Bn. YORKSHIRE REGT.

Instructions regarding War Diaries and Intelligence Summaries are contained in F. S. Regs., Part II. and the Staff Manual respectively. Title pages will be prepared in manuscript.

Place	Date	Hour	Summary of Events and Information	Remarks and references to Appendices
14 B15	21/10/16		The Bn took over the A.F.F.L. & NB SEC 207–14/31's relieving the 21st Bn Middlesex Regt. "D" Coy occupying the front line from B.O.Y.A.U.47 to B.O.Y.A.U.52, "A" Coy from B.O.Y.A.U.52 to B.O.Y.A.U.61 "B" & "C" coy respectively being in Support. Both Front & Support lines were in a bad condition especially the latter which required much work to put it in anything like order. No casualties occurred on this date.	
— Do —	22/10/16		Enemy has been very quiet up to the present has shown very little activity. We had no casualties	
— Do —	23/10/16		Enemy still inactive & no casualties occurring. The men have been working very hard repairing trenches	
— Do —	24/10/16		Up to the present the Bn has experienced a very quiet time	

WAR DIARY or INTELLIGENCE SUMMARY

13th (SERVICE) Bn. YORKSHIRE REGT.

Army Form C. 2118.

Place	Date	Hour	Summary of Events and Information	Remarks and references to Appendices
14 B/15	24.10.16		Only sending over a few S hells & Rifle Grenades. M.02.3.6.5. p.o. of 10 Redfords & Coy was wounded by one of the latter.	
—Do—	25.10.16		On this date D coy were ordered to carry out a raid on the German Trenches from M.31.A.6.11.89. to H.31.6.13.63. To secure two prisoners for identifications & a M.G. reported to be in the enemy line at or about H.31.6.15.70. Strength 3 off & 50 men. This raid is postponed until night of 26/27 Oct. 1916	
—Do—	26.10.16		The raid mentioned yesterday is cancelled on account of the Bn being relieved in this SECTION by the 12th Royal Fusiliers. Orders were received that the Bn when relieved would proceed to LES B7 & 2 B's & would be billeted in AREA 13	
LES B7 & 2 B's	15/10/16 to 7/16		The Bn moved from 14 B15 where it had only 2 Casualties during the eight days tour, to LES B7 & 2 B8 & occupied the same billets as the last time it was stationed there	

Army Form C. 2118.

WAR DIARY
or
INTELLIGENCE SUMMARY. 13th (SERVICE) Bn. YORKSHIRE REGT.

(Erase heading not required.)

Place	Date	Hour	Summary of Events and Information	Remarks and references to Appendices
LES BREBIS	28/7/16		The men were bathed cleaned up on this date. orders having been received that the Division would move on the 29th to AREA B. The 121st Brigade moving to BRUAY via NOEUX LES MINES.	
BRUAY	29/7/16		The Bn moved to BRUAY on this date. A coy leaving 2FS B72 B13 at 6AM other coys at 15 minute intervals. 2 Platoons at 1 minute intervals until clear of NOEUX LES MINES. When the Bn was formed up & marched to BRUAY arriving there about 12 NOON where the men occupied very comfortable billets orders were received that the Brigade would march to ROAD JUNCTION HOUDAIN 7.33.c.3.4. From this point the Bn marched independently to billets VIZZERNS-18 7 m 21 N	
VIZZERNS HOUDAIN			The Bn arrived about 1-15 at this place & occupied billets in an farm building. Headquarters being at the Chateau	

Army Form C. 2118.

WAR DIARY
or
INTELLIGENCE SUMMARY. 13th (SERVICE) Bn. YORKSHIRE REGT.

(Erase heading not required.)

Place	Date	Hour	Summary of Events and Information	Remarks and references to Appendices
VILLERS BRULIN	31/10/16		The Bn. continued training under any arrangements. The new Box Respirator which had been issued on the 28th was used for instruction. The men being specially instructed in its use. It was found to be much more comfortable, & breathing much easier than those previously issued.	

P.P. Kirkby,
Lieut. Colonel.
Commdg. 13th (S) Bn. Yorkshire Regiment.

Army Form C. 2118.

WAR DIARY
or
INTELLIGENCE SUMMARY.   13th (SERVICE) Bn. YORKSHIRE REGT.
(Erase heading not required.)

CONFIDENTIAL

Vol 6

WAR DIARY
OF
13th (Service) Battalion Yorkshire Regiment

From 1st November 1916.
To 30th " 1916.

(VOLUME 6)

Army Form C. 2118.

WAR DIARY
or
INTELLIGENCE SUMMARY.
13th (SERVICE) Bn. YORKSHIRE REGT.

(Erase heading not required.)

Instructions regarding War Diaries and Intelligence Summaries are contained in F. S. Regs., Part II. and the Staff Manual respectively. Title pages will be prepared in manuscript.

Place	Date	Hour	Summary of Events and Information	Remarks and references to Appendices
VILLERS-BRULIN	1/7/16		The Battn. continued training under Company arrangements, special attention being given to box respirator drill. On this day orders were received that the Battn. would proceed to ROSIERE leaving at 8.30 am. on the following day	
ROSIERE	2/7/16		On this day the Battn. left VILLERS BRULIN at 8.30 am and marched to ROSIERE arriving there at 12 noon. Billets were in farm buildings and not very comfortable	
ROSIERE	3/7/16		Work was carried out under Company arrangements. Rifle exercises, Physical training and inspection. Orders were received that the Brigade would leave on the following day and march to the area NEUVILLETTE - BARLY - DOUTREBOIS (½ mile) - RANSART.	
NEUVILLETTE	4/7/16		The Battn. formed up at 9.50 am in column of route ready	

2353 Wt W2544/1454 700,000 5/15 D. D. & L. A.D.S.S./Forms/C. 2118.

Army Form C. 2118.

WAR DIARY
or
INTELLIGENCE SUMMARY.   13th (SERVICE) Bn. YORKSHIRE REGT.

(2)

Instructions regarding War Diaries and Intelligence Summaries are contained in F. S. Regs., Part II and the Staff Manual respectively. Title pages will be prepared in manuscript.

Place	Date	Hour	Summary of Events and Information	Remarks and references to Appendices
NEUVILLETTE	4/7/16		The Battn formed up at 9.50 am in column of Route and moved off at 10 am en route for NEUVILLETTE, this place being reached about 12.30 pm. The afternoon was spent in having a clean up. Orders were received for the Battn to move to CANDAS on the following day.	
CANDAS	5/7/16		The Battn left NEUVILLETTE passing starting point cross roads at M in LA CLOSERIE FM at 4.54, and arrived at CANDAS about 12.30 pm. In this area the billets were quite good.	
CANDAS	6/7/16		Training was carried on under Coy arrangements.	
CANDAS	7/7/16		Battn paraded at 8.30 am and marched out to the training area. W & S of head. CANDAS – GEZAINCOURT for Coy	

Army Form C. 2118.

WAR DIARY
or
INTELLIGENCE SUMMARY.   13th (SERVICE) Bn. YORKSHIRE REGT.

(Erase heading not required.)

(3)

Instructions regarding War Diaries and Intelligence Summaries are contained in F. S. Regs., Part II. and the Staff Manual respectively. Title pages will be prepared in manuscript.

Place	Date	Hour	Summary of Events and Information	Remarks and references to Appendices
CAMPDAS (CONTINUED)	7/1/16		Company training in the morning and Bath training, Advanced guards & Outposts after dinner. Owing to weather being unfavourable the latter part of programme was not carried out.	
CAMPDAS	8/1/16		It was intended to carry out previous days programme but weather was again very bad and prevented outside work.	
CAMPDAS	14/1/16		Training was continued on the above lines to this date when orders were received that the Battn would move to VILLERS L'HOPITAL.	
VILLERS — L'HOPITAL	15/1/16		The Battn arrived at VILLERS L'HOPITAL at 3.15 PM & were billeted in stables & barns	
DO	16/1/16		Training was carried out under Coy arrangements on the open ground south of the village on this date &	

WAR DIARY
or
INTELLIGENCE SUMMARY. 13th (SERVICE) Bn. YORKSHIRE REGT.

(Erase heading not required.)

Army Form C. 2118.

Place	Date	Hour	Summary of Events and Information	Remarks and references to Appendices
Nr NEUVILLETTE	17/4/16		The Battn. with the 12TH SUFFOLK REGT marched to this place under the command of Col. EARDLEY-WILMOT. The men were very comfortably billeted.	
SUS-ST-LEGER	18/4/16		The Battn. together with the 121ST Machine Gun Coy. & 135th Field Ambulance formed a column under the command of LT-COL B G BAKER & marched to this village. Advance guard & Rear Guard was carried out by D & E Coys respectively on the way.	
SUS-ST-LEGER	20/4/16		On this day the Battn. practised the "Attack" & "Defence". In these operations Pickets & the methods of dealing with them were practised in the afternoon & having the men were practised under Coy. arrangements in "Forming up for tasks".	

Army Form C. 2118.

WAR DIARY
or
INTELLIGENCE SUMMARY.
13th (SERVICE) Bn. YORKSHIRE REGT.

(Erase heading not required.)

(5)

Place	Date	Hour	Summary of Events and Information	Remarks and references to Appendices
SUS-ST-LEGER	21/11/16		On this day, this morning was spent in carrying out the "Attack" by Coys. & the use of & action to be taken against "Pickets" was practised & explained. In the afternoon & evening "Outposts by Day & by night" were carried out by Companies	
DOULLENS	22/11/16		On this day the battln. moved to DOULLENS arriving there about 12.30 PM. Coys. were at 200 yds intervals owing to the number of halts on the Road.	
BERTENCOURT LES-DOULLENS	23/11/16		On this day the battln. moved from DOULLENS to this village. Coys. marched at 200 yds interval on account of the number of halts on the Road. minimum halts took place owing to the number of halts ahead.	
FRANCIERES	24/11/16	4 PM	On this day the Battln. marched to this village arriving about 4 PM. Dinner was eaten on the way.	

Army Form C. 2118.

WAR DIARY
or
INTELLIGENCE SUMMARY.

13th (SERVICE) Bn. YORKSHIRE REGT.

(Erase heading not required.)

Place	Date	Hour	Summary of Events and Information	Remarks and references to Appendices
VILLERS-AU-BOIS	11/6		The Battn. marched to this place arriving at 10.30 am, the remainder of the day was spent in cleaning up. Returns of Boots & Clothing etc of a kind was made on account, billets which were in a very filthy condition.	
"	20/6		On this date Training was earnestly taken up. The following days the following work was carried out. Infantry & Section Training, Fire Education & Control, Rapid Loading, Handling of Arms, Physical Drill, Bayonet Fighting, extended order Drill, Digging trenks, Care of Arms, Boots, Clothing etc, Practise in putting on Box Respirators in day time & at night, Instruction of Platoon in Outposts, Advance & Rear guards, Consolidation of ground gained, French & German Warfare, Platoons were instructed also in Diamond Formation, Wood Fighting, am N.C.Os about was Issued & Instruction given in Map Reading, Short Messages, Guards, duties, F.S. Regts, etc in addition to the above the teaching of Signallers, Bombers, L.M. Gunners, & Snipers was carried out in the afternoon	

Army Form C. 2118.

WAR DIARY
or
INTELLIGENCE SUMMARY. 13th (SERVICE) Bn. YORKSHIRE REGT.
(Erase heading not required.)

Place	Date	Hour	Summary of Events and Information	Remarks and references to Appendices
	31/1/16		On the date a draft of 38 other ranks arrived.	

B.B. Baker
Lieut-Colonel
Commdg 13th Yorkshire Regt

Army Form C. 2118.

WAR DIARY
or
INTELLIGENCE SUMMARY.
13th (SERVICE) Bn. YORKSHIRE REGT.

(Erase heading not required.)

Vol 7

CONFIDENTIAL.

WAR DIARY
OF
13th (S). Battalion Yorkshire Regiment.

FROM 1st December 1916.
TO 31st " 1916.

(VOLUME 7).

Army Form C. 2118.

WAR DIARY
or
INTELLIGENCE SUMMARY.   13th (SERVICE) Bn. YORKSHIRE REGT.
(Erase heading not required.)

Place	Date	Hour	Summary of Events and Information	Remarks and references to Appendices
VIZZERS BOCAGE A122S	1/12/16		Training was continued as on previous 8 days whilst stations at this place. Men parading in full marching order for the first time, but since the training commenced this was continued until the 8th Dec when orders were received that the whole of the Transport would proceed to the IV Corps MIDDLE AREA by March Route, the Remainder of the Bn. by Train.	
-DO-	8-9/12/16		On this date the Transport moved as above under the Brigade Transport officers & halted for the night at ST GAUVER and following day they proceeded to camp 124. orders were received that the Bn. would proceed by Train entraining at LONGPRÉ STATION.	
SHILLY LAURETTE	11/12/16		The Bn. paraded at 5-25 am & marched at 6 Longpré Station & entrained leaving at 8-30 am passing through AMIENS	

WAR DIARY
or
INTELLIGENCE SUMMARY

Army Form C. 2118.

13th (SERVICE) Bn. YORKSHIRE REGT.

Place	Date	Hour	Summary of Events and Information	Remarks and references to Appendices
SATURDAY LAMCORD	4/12/15		Arriving at the detraining station EDGE HILL at 12.30 marching to this place & arriving about 5.30 p.m. In this place the Bn. was encamped in Hutments, which were very comfortable & were most preferable to the Billets the men had been used to during the time the Bn. had been on the move. Many improvements are required as outside the huts there are no footpaths & the men are up to the ankles in mud. The officers were all billeted in one Hut, where they all slept & fed. A Bn. mess was formed, this being the first time they had all been together since coming to this country.	
–DO–	12/11/6		On this date work was commenced on improving the camp under Lieut Jennings, which was very necessary as the Bn. were the first British Troops to occupy the camp, which had not been left very clean. Drains were constructed made	

Army Form C. 2118.

13th (SERVICE) Bn. YORKSHIRE REGT.

WAR DIARY or INTELLIGENCE SUMMARY
(Erase heading not required.)

Place	Date	Hour	Summary of Events and Information	Remarks and references to Appendices
SAILLY LAURETTE	12/12/16		roads & paths were improved by the laying down of chalk & french boards. One hut was made into a bath house where the men were enabled to have a very necessary bath & change of clean underclothing. Also another hut was turned into a sick bay where men were able to lay up for a few days instead of being sent to the field ambulance, thus saving men from being sent to a casualty clearing station, where they would have probably been sent to the Base.	
-DO-	13/12/16		Training was continued on the lines as laid down at Villers Sous Ailly, one Coy being left in camp daily to work on improvements & find all details.	
-DO-	15/12/16		On this date a Headquarters Coy was formed under command of Lieut. C.A. Wallis all specialists of the Bn & H.Q. N.C.O's men were posted to this Coy	

Army Form C. 2118.

WAR DIARY
or
INTELLIGENCE SUMMARY

13th (SERVICE) Bn. YORKSHIRE REGT.

(Erase heading not required.)

Place	Date	Hour	Summary of Events and Information	Remarks and references to Appendices
SAIZY LAURETTE	2/2/16		On this date fighting Platoons were formed. All Platoons in the Bn being self contained as regards specialists etc. This arrangement has proved very satisfactory. All officers have to be trained in the Lewis machine gun, bombing & all specialist work.	
-DO-	28/2/16		On this date competitions were arranged with the 12 th Suffolk Regt. 8 Boxing Bouts were arranged. The Bn winning 4 of them & the Suffolks winning 4. Corporal 124 Ruben gave a prize of £100 fres to the winner of these events	
-DO-	24/2/16		On this date a competition for Platoon Drill was arranged between the two Bns. No 6 Platoon representing the Bn who were beaten by the Suffolk Platoon. The Bn was also beaten by the same Bn in a bombing competition. Brigadier General Campbell C.M.G. D.S.O. being Judge. In the afternoon the Bn Representative Team beat the	

WAR DIARY
or
INTELLIGENCE SUMMARY.

Army Form C. 2118.

13th (SERVICE) Bn. YORKSHIRE REGT.

Place	Date	Hour	Summary of Events and Information	Remarks and references to Appendices
SAILLY LAURETTE	24/12/16		Suffolks won by H goals to 1. These competitions helped the good feeling between the two Bns which are now working together in place of the 21st Middlesex Regt.	
-DO-	25/12/16		This being Xmas day arrangements were made to give the men a good time. They were provided with an excellent dinner & coy commdts were told in the evening & they all seemed to enjoy themselves very well. In the afternoon competitions for the men were arranged by coy commdrs. A coy Lecture by Private H & C coy Singing competitions by platoons D coy a Clearing competition the C.O. being judge. The officers of the Bn providing the prizes. A divisional working party was formed on this date 50 men under Capt J R Stewart were despatched to join this 13th.	

Army Form C. 2118.

WAR DIARY
or
INTELLIGENCE SUMMARY. 13th (SERVICE) Bn. YORKSHIRE REGT.

(Erase heading not required.)

Place	Date	Hour	Summary of Events and Information	Remarks and references to Appendices
SAILLY LAURETTE	26/12/16		On this date orders were received that the N.O.I. would relieve the 33rd Division & the 121st Brigade would move into Divisional Reserve on 27th inst	
SUZANNE CAMP 17	27/12/16		On this date the Bn. moved by march route to this place which is a hutted encampment & requires very much improvement. This is the first time the Bn. has been in huts since leaving 14.10.15.	
-Do-	28/12/16		On this date camp improvement was commenced, drains & paths require much improvement as the camp is in a very bad state the mud being very deep in some places to the R.E. gun fire, some	
-Do-	29/12/16		Camp improvement continued, Coys. not on this work are training in their huts	

Army Form C. 2118.

WAR DIARY
or
INTELLIGENCE SUMMARY.

13th (SERVICE) Bn. YORKSHIRE REGT.

(Erase heading not required.)

Place	Date	Hour	Summary of Events and Information	Remarks and references to Appendices
SUZANNE CAMP 17	30/12/16		On this date a Brigade School was formed under Major T Ryan at this school Courses for Lewis Machine Gunners, Rifulers & General course are arranged. Orders were received that the 121st Brigade would relieve the 120th Brigade on the Right (BOUCHAVESNES) Sector on the night of 31st December 1916. The Bn relieving the 11th N.D. Regt in Brigade Reserve.	
A.23.d 12 Sept Map.	31/12/16		The Bn marched to this place arriving at 1-30 p.m. The Quarter Master Stores & Transport of the 121st Infy Brigade are stationed here. all troops are under command of O.C. Reserve Bn. who at present is the C.O. Lt Colonel B.G. Baker. The Bn occupy Tents & dug-outs, which at present are not very comfortable, but are going to be improved whilst the Bn is in Bde Reserve. The ground is very muddy & is covered by innumerable shell holes.	

BGBaker
Lieut. Colonel
Commdg. 13th Bn Yorkshire Regt.

Army Form C. 2118.

WAR DIARY
or
INTELLIGENCE SUMMARY.

(Erase heading not required.)

Vol 8

CONFIDENTIAL.

WAR DIARY

of

13th (S) Battalion Yorkshire Regiment.

From 1st January 1917.
To 31st " 1917.

(VOLUME 8.)

WAR DIARY
or
INTELLIGENCE SUMMARY

Army Form C. 2118.

13th (SERVICE) Bn. YORKSHIRE REGT.

Place	Date	Hour	Summary of Events and Information	Remarks and references to Appendices
A. 23.D Albert MAP	1/1/17		The Bn was in this place as Bn in Reserve until night of 4th/5th Jany 1917 when orders were received that the Bn would relieve the 12th Suffolk Regt in the Right Sub Section (BOUCHAVESNES NORTH)	
Bouchavesnes North	5/1/17		On this date the Bn relieved the 12th Suffolk Regt in this sector. The relief was reported complete by 10-30 p.m. night of 4/5 Jany. A coy being the right front line coy B 13 Bty left front coy C coy Suffolk coy D coy Reserve coy at ANDOVER. In this sector the trenches were impassable owing to heavy rains which caused the trenches to fall in. The only way of getting to the front line was by going over the top of the line was held by a series of posts, which had to be made into dry standings everywhere being very muddy, these dry standings were very difficult to make, owing to material having to	

WAR DIARY
or
INTELLIGENCE SUMMARY

Army Form C. 2118.

13th (SERVICE) Bn. YORKSHIRE REGT.

Place	Date	Hour	Summary of Events and Information	Remarks and references to Appendices
TRENCHES NORTH OF YPRES	5/11/17		be carried about 3 miles overland, all movement could only be done at night. The C.O. Lt Col Baker whilst visiting the Front Line had a runner W.3348 Pte Hitching of E. A. Coy killed immediately behind him when going from A to B Coy by a sniper.	
do	6/11/17		On this date C & D Coys changed over to going to reserve & B to Support. There were no casualties	
do	7/11/17		On this date "C" Coy relieved A & D relieved B Coy in the Front Line. During the day the telephone wire was cut by no. 16 Bombardment thus cutting off communication between B.H.Q. & the Front Line. This was repaired during the night & an officer wire laid which was found very useful as the wire was again cut, but communication was cut on the 2nd line.	

WAR DIARY
INTELLIGENCE SUMMARY

Army Form C. 2118.

13th (SERVICE) Bn. YORKSHIRE REGT.

Place	Date	Hour	Summary of Events and Information	Remarks and references to Appendices
15th NR RAVELSNES NORTH	7/1/17		No 29742 Sgt. T Rowley who was at the 18th School Camp 17 was hit by a machine gun bullet fired from a hostile aeroplane which flew over the camp during the night. He was evacuated the same day. No 24655 Pte W Smith's boy was wounded while carrying rations to the front line.	
-do-	8/1/17		On this date our support line occupied by A Coy was heavily shelled. This Coy had No 29476 Pte G S Cox killed & nine others wounded. On this date the Bn was relieved by 17th Welsh Regt. The Bn moving with the rest of the 121st Bde to bivouac Reserve at Camp 17. The Bn was met at CRAYLETTE by the field kitchens & supplied with hot tea & rum, then marched to MARICOURT PAS where they were met by lorries which conveyed the men to Camp 17 arriving there about 1 am.	
CAMP 17 SUZANNE	9/1/17		In this place the Bn had a much needed rest after	

Army Form C. 2118.

WAR DIARY
or
INTELLIGENCE SUMMARY.   13th (SERVICE) Bn. YORKSHIRE REGT.
(Erase heading not required.)

Place	Date	Hour	Summary of Events and Information	Remarks and references to Appendices
CAMP 17 SUZANNE	9/1/17		A very strenuous day in the Front Line. Repairs to dug-outs & roads was carried out, the men were also bathed at the French Baths & clean underclothing issued. Improvements to the camp were carried out & a certain amount of training on the 18th inst. Orders were received that the 13th would relieve the 12th Bn. on the RANCOURT SECTION during the night of 12th to 13th Jany 1917.	
RANCOURT 12/ ALBANY 1/17			On this date the Bn. relieved 11th K.O.R. Lancaster Regt. in Support at ALBANY. The accommodation for the Bn. was very bad, only small shelters being available. These were improved & new ones made under R.E. supervision, but the surroundings being very muddy and duckboard tracks were made. This place was continually under hostile shell fire but no casualties were sustained during that day. The Bn. was to in support. Orders were received on the 15th inst. to relieve the 12th R.S. & 8th 21st R.F.G. in the RANCOURT RIGHT SUB-SECTION	

2353 Wt. W2544/1454 700,000 5/15 D. D. & L.   A.D.S.S./Forms/C. 2118.

WAR DIARY or INTELLIGENCE SUMMARY

Army Form C. 2118.

13th (SERVICE) Bn. YORKSHIRE REGT.

Place	Date	Hour	Summary of Events and Information	Remarks and references to Appendices
RAMBOUR	16/11/19		On this date the Bn relieved the 12th S'uffs & 21st R E Fus? in the front line & coy being Right front coy, B Left & coy in Support, D in Support & my Reserve. This sector has had toy series of hills. Movement was not possible by day. Rations & water being taken up by the Reserve coy at night. It was very difficult to get about owing to the mud & a number of men had to be pulled out of the hole. Cooking was not possible & hot drinks were provided during this tour, owing to the fact that no mine of importance. Paraffin had been made as in the Boucha'vesnes section. This will cook 2 canteens full of water & were very much appreciated by all. There were three casualties on this date, slightly wounded by shrapnel.	
-do-	17/11/19		On this date B coy in Reserve relieved C coy in support	
-do-	19/11/19		B coy relieved A coy & D relieved B coy in the front line	

WAR DIARY
or
INTELLIGENCE SUMMARY.

13th (SERVICE) Bn. YORKSHIRE REGT.

Army Form C. 2118.

Place	Date	Hour	Summary of Events and Information	Remarks and references to Appendices
RANCOURT	27/9/17		On this date A Coy returned in Reserve, relieved B Coy in Support. Orders were received that the Bn would be relieved by the 12th Suffolks Regt & the proceeding in Reserve in MAUREPAS RAVINE	
Do -	28/9/17		On this date the Bn was relieved by the 12th Suffolks (C 49²). Relief being reported complete by 9-30 p.m. on this date. The Right Coy of the Bn were heavily shelled but sustained no casualties. The Bn arrived at MAUREPAS RAVINE about 1-30 a.m. on the morning of the 29th after a very hard time, during which very frosty & snowy weather prevailed	
MAUREPAS RAVINE	29/9/17		At this place men were rested & cleaned up. This enemy was frequently shelled but only 5 casualties occurring amongst the Regt Transport Horses. Orders were received that the Bn would be relieved by the 19th Lake The 12.1.01.15 etc moving to Camp 17 in Divisional Reserve	

Army Form C. 2118.

WAR DIARY
or
INTELLIGENCE SUMMARY.

(Erase heading not required.)

13th (SERVICE) Bn. YORKSHIRE REGT.

Place	Date	Hour	Summary of Events and Information	Remarks and references to Appendices
CAMP SUZANNE (?)	28/11/17		The Bn arrived at this place 1.30 pm relieving the 19th R.W. Fusiliers. The men were refitted with clothing necessaries. Training was continued, also camp improvements. On this date Col. 16.A Parker took over command of the 13th Inf. Bde during the absence on leave of Brigadier General Campbell C.M.G. D.S.O. The command of the Bn devolving on Major F. Ryan. On the 23rd orders were received that the 40th Divn would be relieved by the 61st Divn & move into Corps Reserve in MIDDLE AREA. The 13th moving to Camp 13.	
CAMP 13	29/11/17		The Bn moved to this place by march Route arriving about 1 pm relieving the 2nd EAST LANCS REG?. All the Camps consist of wooden huts holding about 120 men. At this time of the year they are very black & cold. Such being very the case this Camp is certainly the most uncomfortable	

2353 Wt. W2544/1454 700,000 5/15 D. D. & L. A.D.S.S./Forms/C. 2118.

WAR DIARY
or
INTELLIGENCE SUMMARY

(Erase heading not required.)

Army Form C. 2118.

13th (SERVICE) Bn. YORKSHIRE REGT.

Place	Date	Hour	Summary of Events and Information	Remarks and references to Appendices
CAMP 18	25/1/17		The Bn has recupied up to the present some improvement to roads, which it would intensify the army. It was staying here longer. On 26 inst orders were received that the Bn would proceed to BRAY TO-R-HERE to relieve 2nd DEVON REGt for work at Railhead on 27th inst	
BRAY	27/1/17		The Bn moved to this place on this date by march route arriving about 12.30 p.m. A & B Companies proceeded to BRAY-Tourlers Dump where they were accommodated in huts & are very comfortable. B & D Coys & HQrs are billeted in BRAY. The Bn whilst here are available for work under orders of XV Corps	
-DO-	31/1/17		The Bn has been employed on Railway work during the stay in BRAY. Very little opportunity for training has been found out this return eighty-four men are rejoined	

2353 Wt. W2544/1454 700,000 5/15 D. D. & L. A.D.S.S./Forms/C. 2118

WAR DIARY or INTELLIGENCE SUMMARY

13th (SERVICE) Bn. YORKSHIRE REGT.

Army Form C. 2118.

Place	Date	Hour	Summary of Events and Information	Remarks and references to Appendices
BRAY	30/11/17		-ments & L.M. Gunners which carried out training in this Bn. during 1.O.D.R. returned from a musketry course at POINT REMY. Major T. Ryan acting O.C. was admitted to Hospital. Lieut. (A/Capt.) P. Worthington was promoted acting Captain vice Capt. R. Steward to Div. Works Bn. on 19/11/17. Lieut. W. Scott was promoted acting Captain vice Capt. H.C. Pegg who to Senior Officers Course Aldershot 20/11/17. During the time in the trenches the Bn. Hqrs. sent the smallest number of men returned sick in the Division & was complimented by the Divisional & Brigade Commanders in obtaining this record.	

Kirge. Captain
Commdg. 13th (S)/Bn. Yorkshire Regt.

Army Form C. 2118.

WAR DIARY
or
INTELLIGENCE SUMMARY.
(Erase heading not required.)

Vol 9

CONFIDENTIAL.

WAR DIARY

OF

13th (S). Battalion Yorkshire Regiment.

From. — 1st. February 1917.
To.   — 28th.   "   "   1917.

(VOLUME 9).

Army Form C. 2118.

WAR DIARY
INTELLIGENCE SUMMARY
(Erase heading not required.)

Instructions regarding War Diaries and Intelligence Summaries are contained in F. S. Regs., Part II. and the Staff Manual respectively. Title pages will be prepared in manuscript.

Place	Date	Hour	Summary of Events and Information	Remarks and references to Appendices
BRAY	1st/6		The Battn was stationed at BRAY on these dates	
	10th/6 1917		Between N.C.O & men being employed at Divisional Dump, main of XIV Corps, A & B Coys there billeted in huts at 16 BRAY TURRETT Dump. The work consisted of unloading trains & carrying under R.E. & C.B.D. Coys were billeted in BRAY & were generally on fat. of parties. There is a good stream here where the men were enabled to wash. There in the days previously Regt. under-clothing.	
-do-	15/6/17		Orders were received that the Bn. were to move to camp 21 the men being returned on BRAY by the 14th Supply Co. Southern Highlanders	
CAMP 21	16/6/17		The Bn. moved to this place by march route in full marching order, reliefs being complete about 4-30 p.m. It was impossible to do a great deal in training.	

A 5834 Wt. W4973 M687. 750,000 8/16 D. D. & L. Ltd. Forms/C.2118/13.

WAR DIARY

INTELLIGENCE SUMMARY

(Erase heading not required.)

Army Form C. 2118.

Instructions regarding War Diaries and Intelligence Summaries are contained in F. S. Regs. Part II. and the Staff Manual respectively. Title pages will be prepared in manuscript.

[Stamp: 13th (SERVICE) BATT. YORKS. REGT. ORDERLY ROOM]

Place	Date	Hour	Summary of Events and Information	Remarks and references to Appendices
CAMP 21	11/5/17		Here but news were received that this had to furnish 300 men on Conjunction with the 21st MIDDLESEX Regt who had to find the same number to open Telegins Tullas mine working in two reliefs 24 hours at a time each in Lining were made up and 21st Midd sent 7th. We would consist of mining & employing must of others fatigue duties and to the found for Comps & Depots. It will be the duty for training Our brain. The next hour morning we under instruction & Field duties. This work continues until the night of the 20/21 July when reliefs were secured. Think this 13th July to the night of the 21st July will relieve the 14th Infantry Bde in the NEW CANAL SECTOR the 13th moving into CULLOZ CAMP on 21st July.	

WAR DIARY
INTELLIGENCE SUMMARY

Army Form C. 2118.

Place	Date	Hour	Summary of Events and Information	Remarks and references to Appendices
ALBANY	21/2/17		The Bn moved from camp 21 to the trenches, relieving the 10 P.B.W. Fus. B. Coy occupying ELBERT & LEIPZIG, the remainder of the Bn being in Dug outs in ABBEY WOOD. Here they remained for the night, orders were recd that the Bn would move into the line open the NEW RANDAGE HIGHWAY. See orders appx No 12 & 13 Appy	
MANEDUCH	22/2/17		The Bn relieved the 9th P.R.W. Fus. in the Reserve Sub Sec 2822. relief being complete by 12 M.N. D Coy relieved in right front line Trenches 15 Hy Inf. C Coy in support, B D Coy in Reserve. We spent hours very hard in moving to & then taking up in after relief things recd of 7 & 10 ?	
-DO-	23/2/17		On this date N° 2 5552 P° E.A. Roberts & N° 2 & 324 M. Wilkinson were killed & N° 41926 P° A. G. Wilkinson was wounded during a Trench Mortar barrage of our front line. They all belonged	

Army Form C. 2118.

WAR DIARY
INTELLIGENCE SUMMARY
(Erase heading not required.)

Instructions regarding War Diaries and Intelligence Summaries are contained in F.S. Regs., Part II. and the Staff Manual respectively. Title pages will be prepared in manuscript.

Place	Date	Hour	Summary of Events and Information	Remarks and references to Appendices
BAILLEUL	28/3/17		16 D Coy who occupied the Right of our line R.E. Buckett was at present machine gun numbers in front town to the Bn. Orders were received that the Bn. would be relieved by 12th Suffolk Regt. on night of 2/4 inst.	
— Do —	29/3/17		At about 9.30 pm Enemy opened fire on our front line with artillery & T.Ms. smashing in 2 men of A + 25 of B Coy. The battn. they slightly & they remained at duty. Information received that the Bn. was relieved by 12th Suffolk Regt. relief being completed at 10.30 pm. Bn. H.Q. moved in to Bayencourt and 'A' Coy to L.M. forest. Bn. was moving to the old Bayencourt line to Mantepe. Moving the Bn was occupied by this Suffrs Bn. being reinforced by reinforcements, working parties who actually became part of the support Bn.	
AZAINS	23/3/17		The Bn. received 20th Middlesex Regt. on night of 2/4 – 3/4 in support. The Coys. M.M. + E has been love ended to Bn. who have to change or unwittingly the whole working of this place are very good service approved by the Bayencr	

A 5834 Wt. W.4973/M68   750,000 8/16 D. D. & L. Ltd.   Forms/C.2118/13.

WAR DIARY

Army Form C. 2118.

Place	Date	Hour	Summary of Events and Information	Remarks and references to Appendices
ALBANY	26/9/17		On the 26/9/17 A & C Coys were ordered to move from MAUREPAS RAVINE to BULLIN in HOSPITAL WOOD. This is for shelter had been made in week for the men were in trench.	
-Do-	27/9/17		A & C Coys moved to HOSPITAL WOOD this operation was begun to shelter before proceeding to the front line on night of 28 Sept. Orders were received that the Battn would relieve the 12th 9th Sufft on night of 28th in right Sub Section R.26.2.2.	
RANCOURT	28/9/17		The Batt. relieved the 12th Suffolk Regt in the RANCOURT Right Sub Section on this date. B Coy occupying the right front line A Coy left to B coy in support & D coy observing the S.E. of RANCOURT with their centre at By 10-13 only one casualty occurring the Chamberlain to B coy being slightly wounded from rifle fire.	

R.G. Barn
Major Comdg 13th (S) Bn Yorkshire Regt
28/9/17

WAR DIARY
or
INTELLIGENCE SUMMARY.

Army Form C. 2118.

(Erase heading not required.)

CONFIDENTIAL.

WAR DIARY

OF

13th (S) Battalion Yorkshire Regiment

From – 1st March 1917.
To   – 31st March 1917.

(VOLUME 10).

Vol 10

WAR DIARY
INTELLIGENCE SUMMARY.
(Erase heading not required.)

Army Form C. 2118.

Place	Date	Hour	Summary of Events and Information	Remarks and references to Appendices
RANCOURT	1/3/17		On this date the Bn. was reoccupying the front line in this Sector 76. Coy being on the right & A Coy on the left. About 5.20 a.m. the enemy bombarded our front line & all approaches specially a Sap held by 4 eng. under 2/Lt Smith. Barrage 2.5" of the enemy attempted to raid this Sap. Corpl Smith Sery were held this Sap. Our lewis monitor opened fire. Some of the enemy managed to get in enemy trenches killed & pte. Banks L/Cpl Smith Pte Martin missing. B 29659 Pte. W. Cooke rushed back for help & returned through enemy barrage picked up bombs as he ran & drove the enemy out with bombs. The leader of the raiding party was an Off. & with the assistance of Pte enemy Pte Cooke brought him in after a struggle. Some of the raiding party were seen to be wounded & 4 other dead Bodies were found. One was seen in no mans wire Pte Cooke has been recommended for the D.C.M. for his gallant conduct. The leader who was captured died after being 5 hours in our lines he belonged to the 114th Rgt	

WAR DIARY
INTELLIGENCE SUMMARY.
(Erase heading not required.)

Army Form C. 2118.

Place	Date	Hour	Summary of Events and Information	Remarks and references to Appendices
RANCOURT	1/3/17		The enemy continually shelled our line during the day opposite A.Coy. being killed 2/Lt E.J. Reading & 2 men wounded slightly.	
-DO-	2/3/17		On this date not one suffered seven casualties wounded. No 23399 Pte W.A. Crompion & No 11657 Pte Roberts have since died.	
-D-	3/3/17		On this date only one casualty occured No A2450 Pte J.E. Keek being slightly wounded. Orders were received that the Bn was to be relieved by 12th Suffolk Regt on night of 4/5th march	
-DO-	4/3/17		At 5.15 am on this date our artillery opened fire all along our front. The 8th division on our right attacked towards Trench Fifteen F.M. BOUCHAVESNES. This Bn was detailed to rest all dumps & wounds of wind that been forwarded	

WAR DIARY

INTELLIGENCE SUMMARY

Army Form C. 2118.

Place	Date	Hour	Summary of Events and Information	Remarks and references to Appendices
RANCOURT	4/2/17		The attack of the 8th Division could be seen from our trenches & it was a complete success, all the objectives being gained. During this attack our trenches were under hostile fire the whole time, but we only had ten casualties NO.29310 Pte. Horburne & 5345 Pte. Harrisbent being killed and 2nd Lt. J. Johns & seven men being wounded. The men had a bad time during this tour & were very lucky to get off with so few casualties. The 12th Suffolk Regt. relieved the Bn. relief being completed by 10 P.M. The Bn. moving to MAUREPAS RAVINE in Dv. Reserve.	
MAUREPAS RAVINE	5/2/17		On this date the men were given a days rest to enable them to clean up & take clean underclothing being provided. On this date men were received from the 12th Infy Base moved to relieve by the 23rd Infy Base. The Bn. relieving the 2nd MIDDLESEX REGT at LINGER CAMP. A.30.a.3.6.	

WAR DIARY
INTELLIGENCE SUMMARY
(Erase heading not required.)

Army Form C. 2118.

Place	Date	Hour	Summary of Events and Information	Remarks and references to Appendices
LINGER CAMP	6/3/17 to 13/3/17		The Bn moved to this place by march route. It was a very short march & the men carried full marching order. The Camp consists of NISSEN Huts holding about 35 men. Baths are also provided. The Training of the Bn continued. Bayonet fighting, Physical Drill, Rifle Exercises, close order drill, Bombing with live bombs, L.M. Gun Training, Snipers Practice & Lectures by C.O. being carried out daily. On the 12th a cross country run was arranged.	
-DO-	14/3/17		Orders were received that the 121st Bde would relieve the 119th Bde on 15th march in the CLERY Sector. The Bn being detailed to relieve the 19th Welsh Fusiliers in the Right of the Divisional Front.	
CLERY R. SECTOR	15/3/17		The Bn relieved the 19th R.W. Fus. in this Sector relief being reported complete about 11 p.m. A coy & Coy were right flank rested on the SOMME being the Right	

WAR DIARY
or
INTELLIGENCE SUMMARY

(Erase heading not required.)

Army Form C. 2118.

Place	Date	Hour	Summary of Events and Information	Remarks and references to Appendices
Cley F.Seb.A.7	15/3/17		Coy "B" Lost in the Centre 16 days on the Left, the Bn on our Left being 2nd Middlesex Regt, & the 143rd Bde was on our Right. On the other side of the RIVER SOMME D coy being Support coy at MARET. We had one Casualty while relieving MD 15 2 b 9½ P.½ Lindley 16 Coy being wounded by a Rifle Bullet.	
-Do-	16/3/17		There were no Casualties on this date. The enemy was very active with Rifle grenades Md. Fire, he emptied rounds his own drive in the approach of our posts. Lewis gun very lights actively all night	
-DD-	17/3/16		On this date the enemy was seen in three occasionally hostile artillery fired intermittently during the day. In front of coy was a crater in which the previous M.G. had been	

WAR DIARY
or
INTELLIGENCE SUMMARY.
(Erase heading not required.)

Army Form C. 2118.

Place	Date	Hour	Summary of Events and Information	Remarks and references to Appendices
C2R4.17 R.SECTOR	6/9/17		about it. The C.O. officer had decided that this crater should be taken decisively. About 3 p.m. an officer, 2/Lieut-Manson & ten men rushed over towards the enemy had reached his line on entering the bottom of the barrage caught his fort in a wire game formed which had evidently been laid as a trap exploded slightly wounding all of the party. It is pleasing to note that chiefly all were too hostile to enter the Enemy Line in this Divisional on his retirement from this part of the SOMME, impact on the last report, The Three Front Line coys were stated to be of over occupied, in reference to this the Enemy Line this was now. The two new held by a series of strong points which were constructed. Over original line being the line of resistance. Two platoons of each coy being in the German Line	
			The other two platoons of each coy, being our old line	

WAR DIARY
INTELLIGENCE SUMMARY
Army Form C. 2118.

Place	Date	Hour	Summary of Events and Information	Remarks and references to Appendices
Cleary Q9F8707	17/3/17		The corps were all occupying enemy line by 5 p.m. certain lines of his communications were reconnoitred but nothing could be seen of the enemy except many. The darkness prevented seeing all the distance which showed it was burning down places on his retirement	
DO	18/3/17	act 7-11½ am	Patrols were ordered out at daylight, a patrol of D coy reached Mt St Quentin, this officer was the night out - warned positions occupied by the 7th Dn this date. D coy under Capt D Scott were detailed to occupy Bussieu & later in the day A coy very wellers Capts W Smyth were detailed to occupy H171 J5 another to just N.W. of PERONNE, both coys forming the rear outpost line. The towns were found to be very much knocked about, but a great deal of material ammunition was left lying about	

WAR DIARY
or
INTELLIGENCE SUMMARY.
(Erase heading not required.)

Army Form C. 2118.

Place	Date	Hour	Summary of Events and Information	Remarks and references to Appendices
CLERY BUT SOMME	14/3/17		On this date A & D. coys were relieved in the outpost line by the 12th Suffolk Regt & 20th Middlesex Regt. Suspecting D coy returning to Quady martin & A coy remaining in Support to the 12th Suffolk Regt. That was the relief day. Our coys by have taken charge of doing culverly work/ revents forward in front of our outpost line.	
-DO-	20/3/17		Three coys (A B & D) were ordered to make a road parallel for traffice. This road runs into the German lines & had not been passable before. A coy are still in Support to 12th Suffolk. Reg.	
LA QUINCONCE	21/3/17		On this date the Bn moved to La Quinconce occupied shelters in old German Trenches. These shelters had to be made by the men themselves. This village was on	
	24/3/17			

WAR DIARY
or
INTELLIGENCE SUMMARY.
(Erase heading not required.)

Army Form C. 2118.

Place	Date	Hour	Summary of Events and Information	Remarks and references to Appendices
QUIVIÈRES	21/3/17	6 pm	The outskirts of PERONNE. This on H.R. being in a building previously occupied by the enemy. The whole Bn. are employed on improvement of roads leading to PERONNE. On the 24th orders were received that the 40th Division would be withdrawn into Corps Reserve & the 13st Bde would be employed I.C. CENTRAL which lies between CLÉRY + Mt. ST QUENTIN & quite adjacent to FEUILLANCOURT.	
FEUILLANCOURT	25/3/17		The Bn. moved to this place spending this to the first time under canvas since arriving in France & quite appreciated by the men. They were at once employed on road improvement from HAUT ALLAINES the CANAL crossing nr. MOISLAINS. These roads were in a very bad state in places but as the Bn. had been working 8 hours daily up to date they are now in splendid condition. The Co. very competently carried out a Tactical Exercise under the Supervision on 31/3/17	

13/Yorks
Commdg 13st Bn. Yorkshire Regt.

Army Form C. 2118.

WAR DIARY
or
INTELLIGENCE SUMMARY.
(Erase heading not required.)

Vol II

CONFIDENTIAL.

WAR DIARY

OF

13th (S) Batt. Yorkshire Regiment,

From — April 1st 1917.
To — April 30th 1917.

(VOLUME II).

WAR DIARY
or
INTELLIGENCE SUMMARY.
(Erase heading not required.)

Army Form C. 2118.

Place	Date	Hour	Summary of Events and Information	Remarks and references to Appendices
FEUILLAU COURT	4/4/17		The Bn remained in this place improving roads until the 4th April when orders were received that the Bn would move to MANANCOURT remaining there one night prior to taking over the right Sector of the Bouchavesnes Front.	
MANANCOURT	5/4/17		The Bn marched to this place & reoccupied bivouacs & tents. Coy commanders reconnoitred the front to be taken over tomorrow 6th April.	
REF 67c SE 6/4/17 W.3.4.9			The Bn relieved the 1st Lincoln Regt in the front line. A Coy on right, C Coy on left, B Coy in support, D in reserve. The Front Line consists of numerous 3 Bn right & 4 on left. The 21st Middlesex Regt held the left Sector. No casualties occurred on this date.	

WAR DIARY
or
INTELLIGENCE SUMMARY

(Erase heading not required.)

Army Form C. 2118.

Place	Date	Hour	Summary of Events and Information	Remarks and references to Appendices
REF 57c. S.E. W.3.A.9.	8/4/17		On this date Lieut C.F. Jennings was killed by a sniper who were very active. From Gouzeaucourt also Pts. Melvin, Draper & Fowler were wounded from rifle fire.	
—DO—	9/4/17		On this date a minor operation was carried out by the 21st Middlesex left on our left. The bn had to assist by sending out two fighting patrols under 2/Lieuts Miller & Rolph. The operation commenced at 3 p.m. Our platoons went over the tops left to time & at once came under enemies fire. The right platoon carried out their work without a casualty, but the left platoon came up against one of the enemies strong points & Lieut. Rolph being wounded in the left & Ptes Bell & Burton also being wounded. The work of these platoons was carried out skilfully & greatly	

WAR DIARY
or
INTELLIGENCE SUMMARY.
(Erase heading not required.)

Army Form C. 2118.

Place	Date	Hour	Summary of Events and Information	Remarks and references to Appendices
REF 57c SF	9/4/17		assists the 21st Middlesex Regt to obtain their first objective, with few casualties, but later on in the day their casualties were over 100. On this day Pte Alsop was killed & Pte Prout has since died of wounds. There also six men wounded, all by shell fire.	
-DO-	10/4/17		On this date Pte Pitcock & Pte Neville were wounded by shell fire. The former being hit on the arm with a dud shell. This man had on the previous day carried a message under fire, Pte Lockwood who was with him having the butt of his rifle struck by a bullet.	
-DO-	11/4/17		One casualty occurred on this date, Pte Hardaker being wounded by shell fire. Orders were received that the two wounds be relieved by the 2nd Northampton Regt on the night of 11/12 April.	

WAR DIARY
INTELLIGENCE SUMMARY

Army Form C. 2118.

Place	Date	Hour	Summary of Events and Information	Remarks and references to Appendices
FINS	12/4/17		A+D The Bn. less two coys marched outthrows & had to construct shelter round about this place. Very little cover had been left by the enemy when evacuating this place. B+D coys were billeted in/evacuated?/, there shelter being much better than the remainder of the Bn. who were received but owing to the bad time the men. than had in the front line, the CO. decided to give them a rest which was greatly needed.	
-DO-	13/4/17		Work on improvement of roads was carried out until 3 pm when orders were received that the Bn. would relieve the 12th Suffolk Regt in support by 6 p.m. This was carried out. Bn. H.Q. with B+D Coys occupying DESART WOOD A+D coys in sunken Road	

WAR DIARY

(Erase heading not required.)

Army Form C. 2118.

6.

Place	Date	Hour	Summary of Events and Information	Remarks and references to Appendices
ELVERDI	24/4/17		Received that the Bn would proceed to DESANT WOOD forthwith & come under the orders of O.C. 119 Bde. The 119th were to have been carrying out an attack on VIDLEY Place between the two Bns & was to give support to the 119th Bde. During the day news was received that the 10% would retire the S.W. B° of the 119th who were in support at GINCHY CROSS, would take over the main line of resistance from them. During the evening orders were received that the 6th, 14th & 18th of the 120th Bde would relieve the 6th, 14th & 18th of the 120th Bde which had been taken over by the 120th Bde.	
VIDLEY PLOUTH	25/4/17		The Bn relieved the 14 A.H.L.I. in this place, which on the previous day had been recaptured by the enemy. The 21st MIDDLESEX REG' remained in the West SECTOR of the 120th BDE, The 15th N.Z.B. the 17th WELSH REG' of the 119th BDE being on our right.	

WAR DIARY or INTELLIGENCE SUMMARY

Army Form C. 2118.

Place	Date	Hour	Summary of Events and Information	Remarks and references to Appendices
VILLERS PLOUICH	25/4		The relief was completed by 11:30 p.m. without incident.	
		1/7	Day keeping the sights on on the left Bn Support Coy in Ridone	
-Do-	26/4		On this date the enemy heavily bombarded this place at 11:15 p.m. + intermittently through the place, but no casualties	
		17	occurred.	
-Do-	27/4		The enemy but up a barrage all round the village of MAEFIL + about COUPIAX being intensest. Hostile	
		4.10 a.m.	aircraft is also very active here on Lewis Guns were in	
		17	friendly in use against AEROPLANES. No other casualties occurred in this relief. Two captures German machine guns were obtained	
			against enemy aircraft.	
-Do-	28/4		HOSTILE ARTILLERY + M.G. very active on this date MR 29 L/C	
		17	RESHMENT 10794 BRADBURN CR 46 23445 Pte a Christian Reid, Killed CPL McNully + 3 other rands slightly wounded	

Army Form C. 2118.

WAR DIARY
or
INTELLIGENCE SUMMARY.
(Erase heading not required.)

Vol 12

CONFIDENTIAL

WAR DIARY

OF

13th (S) Battalion Yorkshire Regiment

FROM — MAY 1st 1917.
TO — MAY 31st 1917.

(VOLUME 12)

WAR DIARY
~~INTELLIGENCE SUMMARY~~

Army Form C. 2118.

Place	Date	Hour	Summary of Events and Information	Remarks and references to Appendices
FINS & DESATZ WOOD	13/4/17		running through Q.34.a.c. to Queens Cross. Two platoons of D Coy holding a strong point at the latter place. 10th & three Coys ready at the disposal of O.C. 12th Suffolk Regt	
DESATZ WOOD	14/4/17 to 19/4/17		Whilst at this place work has been devoted to cleaning up, refits to boots, clothing being carried out. Each night carrying parties having to be found for 12th Suffolk Regt, holding the Front Line. Orders were received that the Bn when relieving the 10th Welsh Regt in EPICOURT where the 121st Bde were in Reserve	
EPICOURT	20/4/17 to 24/4/17		In this place the Bn continued training. Lewis gunners were carried out under G.O.C. for Coy & Coy Commanding two Stokes mortars were also carried out by Vickers guns & Stokes guns, orders were	

WAR DIARY
or
INTELLIGENCE SUMMARY

Army Form C. 2118.

Place	Date	Hour	Summary of Events and Information	Remarks and references to Appendices
Plough	28/4/17		In the late intermittent shelling continued & recommenced very heavy shelling P.M. here. Our reserves retaliating with effect. Enemy are heavily reinforced at BAKER Trench suddenly & 1st of this Brigade surrendered. No 296 Sgt W. Cole wounded & 1st of this Brigade surrendered. No 23226 Pte N.H. Wasser 28899 Pte A.S. Gilbert being killed	
—Do—	29/4/17 19		Heavy shelling continued. Two Stumps resumed to Coys. an artillery on each date. Pte 16 G Baker was slightly wounded but remained at duty. N°23797 Pte Wiscout & Pte Gilling, H.Q. Stayne were killed by the same shell which wounded O.C. "B" Baker. The number of casualties since being in TRENCHES Plough 10 O.R. Killed 2 Officers & 19 O.R's wounded. Orders were received that the Batt would be relieved by 14th K.R.L.I. & would proceed to DESATZ WOOD on night of 1st/2nd May 1917.	

J.W. Sachs Lt Col
Comm'dg 13 Yorks Reg't

Army Form C. 2118.

WAR DIARY
or
INTELLIGENCE SUMMARY.
(Erase heading not required.)

Place	Date	Hour	Summary of Events and Information	Remarks and references to Appendices
MAP Ref FRANCE 57.c.S.E.	1/5/17			
VILLERS PLOUICH			On this date the Bn was still in the front line at this place. Enemy artillery being very active, Bn H.Q. being continually bombarded, in consequence of which H.Q. was moved to the Quarry on W side of the village. Two casualties occurred, M.29.8.3.6. Pte J Snyder being killed & M.29.6.1.9. L.Cpl A Dodd wounded, both by shellfire.	
DESART WOOD	2/5/17 to 6/5/17		On this date the Bn was relieved by the 14th H.L.I. and moved to DESART WOOD where the men were fitted out with clothing & boots. They were also trained at free time. Coys were detailed any day for digging in front line trenches. During this stay in this place, the Coys had to occupy the trenches in the rear main line of resistance in front of QUEENS CROSS. On the night of 6/7 May Bn H.Q. moved to GOUZEAUCOURT WOOD, when orders were received that the Bn would relieve the 14th H.L.I. in VILLERS PLOUICH	

WAR DIARY or INTELLIGENCE SUMMARY.
Army Form C. 2118.

Place	Date	Hour	Summary of Events and Information	Remarks and references to Appendices
VIZZERNO PLOMICH	5/5/17		On this date the Bn relieved the 14th H.L.I. in the Front Line, BN H.Q. being in FIFTEEN RAVINE, A & B Coy occupying the Front Line, C Coy in support, D in Reserve. The 21st MIDDLESEX R.E.Q. being on our Right. The relief was carried out without casualties	
	6/5/17			
	9/5/17		Work was carried out of deepening trenches, turning the whole of the line	
-Do-	10/5/17		On this date at 10.29 P.M. Pte H. Whitall was wounded by shrapnel	
-Do-	11/5/17 to 12/5/17		On this date our Coy relief took place, D relieving A Coy on the right, B relieving C on the left, A moving to support, B Coy to Reserve	
	13/5/17		On 13th orders were received that the 121st Infy Bde were to be relieved by 60th Infy Bde, the Bn being relieved by the [?]	

WAR DIARY
or
INTELLIGENCE SUMMARY.
(Erase heading not required.)

Army Form C. 2118.

3

Place	Date	Hour	Summary of Events and Information	Remarks and references to Appendices
Sot-z LE GRAND	14/5/17		B.n. of Monchi I.E. after relief the Bn moved to Sot-z LE GRAND.	
	22/5/17		The Bn rested for the day at this place. During the night 181st Bde relieved the 85th Infy Bde in the VILLERS GUISLAIN Sector. The Line being held by the 12th SUFFOLK Regt. on Right, 20th MIDDLESEX Reg on the Left. This Bn being the Support relieving the 2nd LINCOLNS REG 2 & 21st MIDDLESEX REG being in Bde Reserve. During this period the Bn was employed on carrying to front line every night. During the day by guns to clothing etc were carried out. Only Casualty occurred during the eight days the Bn was in support. 10246 48. Pte. J Baldwin C. Coy being wounded by shell fire. Orders were received that the Bn would be	

WAR DIARY or INTELLIGENCE SUMMARY

Place	Date	Hour	Summary of Events and Information	Remarks and references to Appendices
			relieved by the 106th Infy Regt. Infy Bde the night of 23/24th May. The MM being relieved by the 119th MGC [?]	
DESART WOOD	23/5 to 25/5/17		On this date after relief the Bn moved to DESART WOOD where they remained until the night of 25/26th when the Bde relieved the 125th Infy Bde in the VILLERS PLOUICH AREA	
VILLERS PLOUICH	25/5/17		On this date the Bn relieved 1/5 K.L. Regt in the front line. A Coy on Right, B on Left, C Coy in support. D Coy in reserve. Before the relief was complete the enemy put up a barrage along the whole Bn front, & shelled the left flank of the 21st MIDD'x Regt who were to take over our right. A platoon of our C Coy reoccupied this post as soon as information was received that [crossed out] enemy. The Barrage we had from preceded two returned the 1/5 K.L. Regt who were still in the trenches	

WAR DIARY
INTELLIGENCE SUMMARY
(Erase heading not required.)

Army Form C. 2118.

5.

Place	Date	Hour	Summary of Events and Information	Remarks and references to Appendices
VILLERS PLOUICH	26 to 29/5/17		had several casualties all wounded. The 21st MIDDLESEX REGt had a number of casualties & had one man 9 a.m. missing. During this period work on continuous front line has been carried out by 12th Suffolk Regt whilst the 7th Bn have been working on a ref. during wire & a relief of immaterial Patrols. On the 29th instant Coy relief of A Coy was carried out.	
-DO-	30/5/17		Inter Coy relief of B & C Coy was carried out. This had twice been in reserve of a number of reports which was to have been carried through by a Coy 2nd East Lancs to moving to new Posts in advance of our present line. The Posts about 300+ were dug by 12th Suffolk Regt under R.E. supervision & wired by this Bn on night of 30/31st. No casualties were incurred during this important work.	

Army Form C. 2118.

WAR DIARY
or
INTELLIGENCE SUMMARY.
(Erase heading not required.)

Place	Date	Hour	Summary of Events and Information	Remarks and references to Appendices
VLETS ROUEN	31/5/17		Work on new huts was continued under Lieut. M. Dun while your turn complete before daylight. No casualties occurred	

Morris,
Lt Colonel
Comdg. 13th (S) Bn Yorkshire Regt.

Army Form C. 2118.

WAR DIARY
or
INTELLIGENCE SUMMARY.
(Erase heading not required.)

Vol. 13

CONFIDENTIAL.

WAR DIARY

of

10th (S) Battalion Yorkshire Regiment

FROM — JUNE 1st 1917
TO — JUNE 30th 1917

(VOLUME 13)

Place	Date	Hour	Summary of Events and Information	Remarks and references to Appendices

WAR DIARY
or
INTELLIGENCE SUMMARY.

Army Form C. 2118.

Place	Date	Hour	Summary of Events and Information	Remarks and references to Appendices
VILLERS-PLOUICH	1st June 1917		On this day the Battalion was still in the lines and continued work of wiring to new front line. The following casualties occurred on this date :- No 42,415 Pte b. Norton — wounded by bullet No 14919 Private W. Bairdmore. No 26517 Pte W. Pontefract. No 29855 Pte J. Henderson — wounded by shell.	
— " —	2nd June 1917		Wiring was again carried out two casualties occurring during wiring operations, No 24613 L/Cpl W. Howard and No 23335 Private F. Hopley both being killed by machine gun fire. The following casualties also occurred on this date :- No 25/64 Pte Bell W., No 26144 L/C Barnes D, No 24844 L/C Weldon D., No 18391 Pte Matsell R., No 33483 Pte Stewart R.H, and No 13661 Pte Bonham W., killed by shell fire. wounded by shell. Orders were received to the effect that the Battalion would be relieved on the night of 2nd/3rd June and would proceed and occupy camp at SOREL-LE-GRAND.	
SOREL-LE-GRAND	3rd June 1917		As per previous orders received the Battalion was relieved by the 18th Battalion Welsh Regiment. The new line of posts contracted by the Battalion was not taken over. The whole of the 121st Infantry Brigade was now in Divisional Reserve.	

Army Form C. 2118.

WAR DIARY
or
INTELLIGENCE SUMMARY.
(Erase heading not required.)

Instructions regarding War Diaries and Intelligence Summaries are contained in F. S. Regs., Part II. and the Staff Manual respectively. Title pages will be prepared in manuscript.

Place	Date	Hour	Summary of Events and Information	Remarks and references to Appendices
SORREL-LE-GRAND	4th July 1917		As the relief was very late the previous night the men had a good rest and duties were confined to cleaning up. Lt. Col. B. G. Baker proceeded on leave. The command of the Battalion was taken over by Capt. J. Margo. 2/Lt. A. N. Humphries assuming the duties of Acting Adjutant.	
-"-	5th July 1917		The first anniversary of the Battalion embarking for active service was celebrated on this date. A concert was given by members of the 136th Field Ambulance and the 17th Battalion Welch Regt. Band played selections. Various games were also indulged in.	
-"-	6th to 10th July 1917		During this period training was carried out on the following lines:- Steady Drill - Handling of Arms - Musketry - Bayonet Fighting - Bombing - Piquet duties - patrols by platoons by night, matching by compass - Lectures. On the 6th inst. Lieut. (T/Capt) J. F. Worthington and 2/Lt. A. R. Watts left the Battalion to proceed on probation to Kent G. H. Staying Depôt. Reviews and inspections of various kinds were provided for the men on the route of the Then Company Commanders.	

A 58.4   Wt. W4473 M687 750,000 8/16 D. D. & L. Ltd. Forms/C.2118/13.

WAR DIARY
or
INTELLIGENCE SUMMARY.

(Erase heading not required.)

Army Form C. 2118.

Place	Date	Hour	Summary of Events and Information	Remarks and references to Appendices
SOREL-LE-GRAND	6th June 1917	to 10th June	was as follows :— Inter Coy Bombing Competition — won by "C" Company; Bombing Competition — won by "C" Company; Tent pitching Competition — won by "C" Company; knock out six-a-side football Competition — won by "B" Company. Interoompts sing-songs were arranged most evenings. The weather during this period was very fine and the men had a thorough good rub and plenty of recreation. Orders were received on the 10th inst, that the 91st Infantry Brigade would relieve the 120th Infantry Brigade in the GONNELIEU Sector on the night of 11th/12th inst.	
GONNELIEU Sector W.H.a. 2/c. S.E. 57¢.N.W. 3/c. S.E. 1/40,000	11th to 14th June 1917		The Battalion relieved the 11th Battalion Kings Own Royal Lancs Regt. in Brigade Reserve. Battalion Head Quarters and "B" Company were situated in Gunters Keep on W 4 a and W 3 d. "D" Company were on the Gunter Road in W 6 d. "A" and "C" Coys "C" Company was in R 31 d and X 1 d. in trenches on R 31 d and X 1 d. During this period two and sometimes 3 Companies were working every night in constructing a front line for the 12th Battalion Suffolk Regiment on the Right GONNELIEU sector.	

WAR DIARY
or
INTELLIGENCE SUMMARY.
(Erase heading not required.)

Army Form C. 2118.

Instructions regarding War Diaries and Intelligence Summaries are contained in F.S. Regs., Part II. and the Staff Manual respectively. Title pages will be prepared in manuscript.

Place	Date	Hour	Summary of Events and Information	Remarks and references to Appendices
GONNELIEU Sector N.W.a Map 57cSE 1/20,000	16th June 1917		Inter Company Relief took place on this date. 'D' Company relieving 'A' Company and 'C' Company relieving 'B' Company.	
	16th to 19th June		Working parties were still ## found for the 12th Battalion Suffolk Regiment. On the 19th inst. orders were received to the effect that the Battalion would relieve the 12th Battalion Suffolk Regiment on the Right Sub-sector GONNELIEU on the night of 19th/20th June 1917.	
GONNELIEU Right Sub-sector.	19th June 1917		The Battalion relieved the 12th Bn Suffolk Regiment in the front line 'A' Company took over the Right Front and 'B' Company the Left Front, 'D' Company Right Support 'C' Company Left Support.	
"	20th June 1917 to 21st June 1917		Owing to the bad state of the weather the trenches taken over were very bad, being full of mud and and water and containing practically no shelters for the men. Allowable men was put on improving the condition of the front line. Trench Boards were got up and laid down. Footsteps made and fire bays revetted. Pumps were obtained to pump water from the water logged front of the trenches. Two casualties occurred on this date - No 49331 Cpl I Dawson killed, WC W4973 M68 750,000 8/16 D.D. & L. Ltd. Forms/C.2118/13. Pte A Jarfoot wounded.	

WAR DIARY
or
INTELLIGENCE SUMMARY.
(Erase heading not required.)

Army Form C. 2118.

Place	Date	Hour	Summary of Events and Information	Remarks and references to Appendices
GONNELIEU Right Sect Sector	22nd June 1917		The improvement in the condition of the trenches proceeded steadily. There were three casualties - No 19469 Pte W Bennett killed. No 18912 Pte R Newton and No 23892 Pte Wesley wounded.	
--"--	23rd June 1917		Inter-Company Relief took place on this date. "D" Company relieving "A" Company, and "A" Company relieving "B" Company. A new belt of wire was run out 200 yards in front of the present front line. The wiring was carried out by the R.E. We Battalion furnished covering parties and the whole Battalion to nothing off wiring parties from Corpl Rosser about casualties - No 29801 Pte R Fisher and No 21700 Pte W B Dudley	
--"--	24th June 1917 to 26th June 1917		Work was commenced on digging new front line by the 12th Battalion Suffolk Regiment & parts were started on the 12th Battalion front. The Companies on the line with the help of the two support Coys provided the covering parties and patrols necessary for this, without also carrying parties to the them it was already started by the R.E.'s On the 25th inst was one casualty - No 17616 Pte J B Hawkes, wounded by machine gun bullet. On the 26th inst, orders were received to the effect that the Battalion would be relieved by the 15th Battalion Welsh Regt on	

WAR DIARY
or
INTELLIGENCE SUMMARY.

(Erase heading not required.)

Army Form C. 2118.

Place	Date	Hour	Summary of Events and Information	Remarks and references to Appendices
GOUZEAUCOURT Left Sub-Sector	27th June 1917		On night of the 27/28th June 1917. On relief the Battalion proceeded to bivouac situated midway between FINS and DESSART WOOD taking over the accommodation previously occupied by the 17th Battalion Welsh Regiment.	
FINS	28th June 1917		Baths were allotted to the Battalion on this date and cleaning up generally was carried out	
"	29th June 1917		The camp was afterwards reorganised on as more convenient manner and a certain amount of time devoted to Rifle Drill - Inspection of Gas Appliances - Practice and Hand Grenade - Bombing. Warning Orders were received that the Brigade was going to country in two Brigade Groups and the VILLERS GUSLAIN Sector on the 2nd/3rd July. 2/Lieut. G.H. Perkins joined the Battalion as a reinforcement this day	

WAR DIARY
or
INTELLIGENCE SUMMARY.
(Erase heading not required.)

Army Form C. 2118.

Place	Date	Hour	Summary of Events and Information	Remarks and references to Appendices
FINS	30th June 1917		The Divisional Baths at FINS were allotted to the Battalion on this date. This is the first time since the Battalion has been in the Country that they had an opportunity in this kind of recreation, which is greatly appreciated by all ranks.	

Hugo Captain,
O.C. "A" Coy Yorkshire Regiment

Monday 13th

WAR DIARY
or
INTELLIGENCE SUMMARY.

Army Form C. 2118.

CONFIDENTIAL

WAR DIARY

OF

13TH (S) Battalion Yorkshire Regiment

From — JULY 1ST 1917
To — JULY 31ST 1917

(VOLUME 14)

WAR DIARY or INTELLIGENCE SUMMARY

Army Form C. 2118.

Place	Date	Hour	Summary of Events and Information	Remarks and references to Appendices
FINS	1st July 1917		On 1st July 1917 orders were received that the 1st/1st and 1st/3rd Infantry Brigade would relieve the 35th Division on night of 1st/2nd July, in the GUISLAIN Sector, PAUCHÉ WOOD and VILLERS GUISLAIN being do'd, weather very little work was done on this day.	
X.3.A.6.3 Ref to S.E. Cor. Sheet 51 b/100,000 VILLERS-GUISLAIN	2nd July 1917		Tents were struck and preparations made for the evening tour of duty in the line. The Battalion relieved the 20th Battalion Lancashire Fusiliers in the Right Out-Post, VILLERS-GUISLAIN sector. On the way to the line a fuse from the main from to the horse which forms a rather a good head in to the wiring gave and the line taken to get ready for two weeks to be completed in the meanwhile. The Battalion were disposed as follows:— "A" Company were in the Keep in Right front. "B" Company to Company in the Keep no Left front. "C" Company in Support at VILLERS-GUISLAIN. "D" Company in Reserve at HEUDICOURT, forming part of Composite Battalion in Brigade Reserve. Battalion Head Quarters were in HIGH	

WAR DIARY

Army Form C. 2118.

Place	Date	Hour	Summary of Events and Information	Remarks and references to Appendices
VILLERS-GUISLAIN 2nd Bn. East Yorks 61st Inf. Bde 5th Div X.9.d.5.1.	July 1917 3rd		STREET. On the 3rd July the whole Brigade front was re-adjusted. The 20th Bn Middlesex Regt on the left extended their front to include HIGH STREET. The Battalion extended its front to include the whole of STOTAR AVENUE not inclusive. After the re-adjustment the situation was as follows – Each of the 4 Battalions had one Company in the front line; one Company in Support; one Company in Brigade Reserve and Battalion HQ. One Company in local Battalion front Brigade Reserve. Here the front line Aton HIGH STREET "A" Company exclusive to STOTAR AVENUE, and front line "B" Company. HQ and Battalion HQ front at ROBERTS AVENUE and their quarters close South of GLOSTER ROAD. To my were in Support in GLOSTER ROAD. "D" 3 Platoons in VILLERS-GUISLAIN, and "D" 1 Platoon Reserve in Southern part of Brigade Reserve in Company formed part of Brigade Reserve. BHQ moved to GLOSTER ROAD X.9.a.5.1. HEUDICOURT.	

WAR DIARY
or
INTELLIGENCE SUMMARY

Army Form C. 2118.

Place	Date	Hour	Summary of Events and Information	Remarks and references to Appendices
VILLERS-GUISLAIN X9 d 51	4th 9th July		During the period the trenches remained in the same line. A great deal of work was necessary in the front trenches as in a bad condition. There were no attacks except for the unusual number of snipers and a warning to the bad weather the trenches were in a very bad state of confusion. There was a very bad spell at times in the days and the weather was continually shelled by our front - made the lives very uncomfortable. By the night of the 8th the trenches had been altered, traverses had been put in and front boards laid, had the top of the trenches strengthened & running some men in. On the 9th the trenches were thoroughly cleaned. The troops were taken to B.H.Q. in lorries and billeted. During the period Pte Beckett was slightly wounded. No 2349 Pte Beckett was slightly wounded.	
	9th		Relief took place. "A" Coy relieved by "13" Company, "B" Coy relieved by "C" Company, "C" Company "B" Company relieved by "A" Company.	
	10th		On this date orders were received that the Brigade Front was to be relieved.	

WAR DIARY / INTELLIGENCE SUMMARY

Army Form C. 2118.

Place	Date	Hour	Summary of Events and Information	Remarks and references to Appendices
VILLERS-GUISLAIN X.9.d.5.1	10th		re-adjusted. The front line was to be held by two Battalions in line, one Battalion in support and one to take over on the night of 11/12th in Reserve.	
VILLERS-GUISLAIN X.3.a.6.3	11th to 15th		On the night of 11th/12th Inst, the Battalion relieved in accordance with instructions received, by the 12th Bn. Suffolk Regiment. The Battalion proceeded to a number of huts on the Gouzeaucourt/Villers-Guislain Rd. On the way there one man was killed by shell fire and five a few minutes later, also No. 29488 Pte G. Simpson was killed at the same time. Those killed in to-day occupied by one of the Battalion being No. 29568 Sgt. S. Wilkinson, No. 29578 L/Cpl. Bradley B. & wounded No. 23/75 Pte. J. Smith and No. 29689 Pte. D. Sanders. On relief the Battalion moved into support, occupying the following positions:— "A" Coy. in GLASS STREET (read through X.fin.) "B" Coy. in GLOSTER ROAD. "C" Coy. in the Trenches K19 (fin) x 15.b. Two platoons of "D" Coy in HIGH STREET and two platoons in CEMETERY ROAD. The Battalion remained in support while	

Army Form C. 2118.

WAR DIARY
or
INTELLIGENCE SUMMARY.
(Erase heading not required.)

Instructions regarding War Diaries and Intelligence Summaries are contained in F.S. Regs., Part II. and the Staff Manual respectively. Title pages will be prepared in manuscript.

Place	Date	Hour	Summary of Events and Information	Remarks and references to Appendices
VILLERS-GUISLAIN X.3.d.6.3.	14th to 15th July		The nights of the 14th/15th and working parties were found every night for from the Battalion.	
VAUCELLETTE FARM.	16th July		On the night of 15/16th July the Battalion was relieved by the 21st Battalion Middlesex Regiment and moved into Brigade Reserve at HEUDICOURT and VAUCELLETTE FARM. B.H.Q. "C" and "D" Coys. moved to VAUCELLETTE FARM and "A" and "B" Coys. to HEUDICOURT. "A", "B" Coys. were allotted the northern half of HEUDICOURT to man.	
"	17th		Baths were allotted to B.H.Q. "C" and "D" Coys. in the huts in HEUDICOURT.	
VILLERS-GUISLAIN X.9.d.5.9	18/19th July		On the night of 18/19th July the Battalion relieved the 10th Battalion Suffolk Regiment in Right Sub sector of VILLERS-GUISLAIN sector. Just before proceeding up the line the Companies were lined up outside B.H.Q. and Brigadier-General Brand DSO, CMG, Commdg. 76th Brigade, presented the ribbon of the CROIX-DE-GUERRE to 13590 Sgt. W.J. Brown of "B" Coy. for his gallant conduct during a raid on the enemy trenches on 1.10.16. The K.6.6 was

T.134. Wt. W708-776. 500000. 4/15. Sir J. C. & S.

WAR DIARY

Army Form C. 2118.

Place	Date	Hour	Summary of Events and Information	Remarks and references to Appendices
VILLERS-GUISLAIN x 9 d 6.1	18th July 1917 to 19th July 1917		Previously been awarded the D.C.M. Dispositions of the Battalion in the line were as follows:— "D" Company went in the line on Right front — "B" Coy went in the line on Left front — "A" Coy were Right Support Company — "C" Company were Left Support Company. The following casualties occurred on this date:— No 10404 Pte A. Roe. Killed — No 30446 Pte J. Rumsey wounded. No 35408 Pte Toy D., No 11807 Pte Joghen J.	
— " —	20th to 21st		The following casualties occurred during this period:— No 35593 Pte J. W. Brayton Killed and No 9371 Pte M. Samuel. — No 24884 Pte J. B. Smith wounded.	
— " —	22nd to 23rd		On the night of the 22nd July "A" Company relieved "D" Company and "B". 16 Company relieved "B" Company in the line. No 11541 Sgt W. Allerton was wounded by a grenade on the 23rd inst. On the 23rd inst. the 13 Blank joined the Bn. as a reinforcement	

WAR DIARY
INTELLIGENCE SUMMARY

Army Form C. 2118.

(Erase heading not required.)

Instructions regarding War Diaries and Intelligence Summaries are contained in F.S. Regs., Part II. and the Staff Manual respectively. Title pages will be prepared in manuscript.

Place	Date	Hour	Summary of Events and Information	Remarks and references to Appendices
VILLERS-GUISLAIN x 9 d 5.1	2/9/17 6/9/17		"D" Company were sent as Right Support during movement in reserve on the dose.	
	25th to 8th July 1917		No casualties occurred on the 25th inst. On the early morning of the 26th inst, the enemy raided our Right Front Company under cover of an intense Barrage and information of this raid was obtained from a German deserter who had been attached to Artillery were quite prepared and put up an exceedingly heavy barrage which inflicted severe losses on the enemy who returning to their lines. The following casualties occurred during the operation :- 15 killed, 6 wounded, and 1 missing E/O Holgate & J.J. McBrown joined the Battalion as reinforcements on the 26th inst. 2/Lt. McBrown proceeded to the Four Kingssorie on the night of the 27/8th inst. during mining operations.	

WAR DIARY or INTELLIGENCE SUMMARY

Army Form C. 2118.

Place	Date	Hour	Summary of Events and Information	Remarks and references to Appendices
VILLERS-GUISLAIN X 9 d 5.	28th to 27th July 1917		out with "A" Company met "B" Company charged out with "A" Company met "B" Company "B" Company.	
— " —	28th to 29th July		There were only three casualties during the period :— No.7961 L/C W. Eaton — No.29664 Pte Revell & and No.33473 Sgt. R. Davis wounded. The N. Yorkshire joined the Bn. as a reinforcement on the 29th.	
— " —	30th to 31st		Work above continued on improving the trenches, and wiring further wire out every night. Inter-company Relief again took place on the 31st inst., "A" Coy relieving "B" Coy and "B" Coy relieving "C" Coy.	

Wigg Major
Commanding 139(S) Bn Yorkshire Regt.

Army Form C. 2118.

WAR DIARY
or
INTELLIGENCE SUMMARY.
(Erase heading not required.)

Vol 15

Confidential

War Diary
of
13th (S) Battn. Yorkshire Regt.
From :- 1st August 1917.
To :- 31st August 1917.
(Volume 15)

WAR DIARY
or
INTELLIGENCE SUMMARY.
(Erase heading not required.)

Army Form C. 2118.

Place	Date	Hour	Summary of Events and Information	Remarks and references to Appendices
Ref Map. 57c S.E. Scale 1/20,000. X.9.d.5.1 VILLERS-GUISLAIN	1st Aug 1917		Artillery on both sides very quiet. No casualties occurred on this sector. Indent was issued to the effect that Mustard would be about the night of the 1st inst by the 20th Battalion Hampshire Evidence as far forth as X.11.a.0.6. sent by the 20th Bn. Middlesex Regiment from X.11.a.0.6. On completion of relief the Battalion Dispositions were as follows :— Battalion Head Quarters } - Vaucellette Farm and "C" and "D" Coys } "A" Company - { Derby Post in Sherwood Lane, X.9.d.55.60 "B" Company - { About York Post in Gloster Road, X.9.d.45.90	1

Army Form C. 2118.

WAR DIARY
or
INTELLIGENCE SUMMARY.
(Erase heading not required.)

Place	Date	Hour	Summary of Events and Information	Remarks and references to Appendices
Poppy Post, Cemetery Road, R.E.7.1.	2nd Aug to 5th Aug 1917		In accordance with Brigade Operation Order the Enquiries Covering was carried out. Under the above i.e. the Battalion moved into Brigade Support relieving the 12th Bn Essex Suffolk Regiment. Dispositions :- Head Quarters :- Poppy Post - R.E.1.1.b. Battalion {"A" & "D" Companies :- Cross Post, X.7.d.50.10.} in support to Right Battalion. {"B" Company :- T.U.3.b. } {"C" :- X.1.b.00.50.} in support to Left Battalion. Improvement of shelters and sanitary conditions - fitting of loops - training in musketry - a.a.t. genral useful work was carried out during the period. Working parties were found nightly for the Front Line Battalions. "C" Company moved to position in Gommelieu	

Army Form C. 2118.

WAR DIARY
or
INTELLIGENCE SUMMARY.
(Erase heading not required.)

Instructions regarding War Diaries and Intelligence Summaries are contained in F. S. Regs., Part II. and the Staff Manual respectively. Title pages will be prepared in manuscript.

Place	Date	Hour	Summary of Events and Information	Remarks and references to Appendices
Front Line near Ytres road L.7.d.	4th Aug 1917 5th Aug 1917		Wood F.26.d.50.40. on the 4th inst.	
Vaucellete Farm	6th Aug to 11th Aug 1917		The Bn. Battalion Madame regained relieved the Battalion in Brigade Support and dispositions on night of 6th inst., were as follows:— Battalion Head Quarters :— Vaucellete Farm. "B" and "C" Company "A" and "D" Companies — Heudicourt The following programme of training was carried out :— Musketry — Rifle and L. Gun Practice on Range — Close Order Drill — Physical Training and Bayonet fighting — Lectures on roads and patrols. The Band also played	

WAR DIARY
INTELLIGENCE SUMMARY

Army Form C. 2118.

Place	Date	Hour	Summary of Events and Information	Remarks and references to Appendices
Wolfare Farm	6th to 7th Aug 1917		7th At Battalions Support by the 10th inst. C.O. M⁴/O. Commanding & Division occupied the Business G.O.C. gave orders for the troops in the trenches to relieve the 12th Battalion of the Regiment.	4
meters m— 16d N0 30.	8th Aug 1917		In the trenches (left sector of Brigade line) Battalion Boundary:- Cain Avenue R81.a 7.4. inclusive to Turner's Quarry, R84. C 10.0. inclusive. Dispositions:- D Company — Right Front Company E " — Left Front Company D " — Right Support Company A " — Left Support Company Artillery activity on either side during [illegible] day & night. They did practically nothing by the night. Good progress made in strengthening our line. A	

Army Form C. 2118.

WAR DIARY
INTELLIGENCE SUMMARY
(Erase heading not required.)

Place	Date	Hour	Summary of Events and Information	Remarks and references to Appendices
Trenches W.21.d.40.30	17th to 21st		Quantity of barbed wire laid down — effected continuous round ... and general work carried out. Wire patrols pushed out in front. Wiring and infantry patrols pushed out towards enemy wire, enemy posts & at Halbotomy Points Seen and noted in condition of Boesinghe the enemy's wire from to from to front of wiring on top proceeding to keep such enemy movement made out at any enemy seen. The Battalion Commander on his visit to the line considered that the garrison and machine gun of the length of frontage held and therefore decided to hold a three company front. "B" Company in reserve not to come into the line on the completion of relief. On completion of relief dispositions were as follows:— "D" Company — Right, Bn Headquarters and 2 platoons in Ellerstone Quarry. "A" Company — Centre, Bn Headquarters with 3 platoons in front system in McVey Street.	

WAR DIARY
INTELLIGENCE SUMMARY

Army Form C. 2118.

Place	Date	Hour	Summary of Events and Information	Remarks and references to Appendices
Somewhere in F.26.d.4.2 & 6.6.	Aug 1917		"A" Company left front trenches with 2 platoons on tactical duties in Gun Support.	6
			"B" Company - did not carry on Kitchen Craters.	
			A Minor Enterprise was carried out on night of 8/9th August 1917:-	
			Objects:- To annoy enemy by throwing rifle grenades & bombs into his line at about T.22 a 9.3 and T.22 a 5.1.	
			To obtain identification.	
			"B" Company carried out the Operation, which was composed of the following parties:-	
			Left Bombing and Covering Party consisting of 2 N.C.O.s and 10 others under 2/Lt S.H. Bacon.	
			Right Bombing and Covering Party consisting of 2 N.C.O.s, two scouts and 10 others, with 2/Lt T. Douch in charge. Rifle grenade & bomb supply, 2 N.C.O.s and 18 others as support Party, consisting of 1 Lewis Gun with 7 N.C.O.s under 2/Lt F.H. Walker.	

Army Form C. 2118.

WAR DIARY
or
INTELLIGENCE SUMMARY
(Erase heading not required.)

Instructions regarding War Diaries and Intelligence Summaries are contained in F.S. Regs., Part II. and the Staff Manual respectively. Title pages will be prepared in manuscript.

Place	Date	Hour	Summary of Events and Information	Remarks and references to Appendices
Railway Hills	11th Aug 1917		The attack left our trenches at midnight. On approaching the enemy wire the scouts reported the enemy working parties approaching the wire. Most of the German wire had been cut, but there were in some places. The parties then advanced and were soon at the line. Warning of party by surprise and a great number were taken prisoner. Examining enemy machine gun to fire on our advance. Our parties then opened rapid fire & kept up rapid firing. The Bangalores, Russian attempts were made, many machine gun rifle fire could not advance the ground of object, and the withdrawal was ordered owing to the enemy of support. Only one casualty. Seven away to the **Brigade Support.** The Battalion moved to the **Brigade Support.** Demolitions as in yesterday's task. A great deal of work was put in on the entrenchment where needed, were repaired with a certain amount of newly-fitted trench clothes and recovered.	
Poperinghe Cemetery to Road X26.C.6	12th Aug 1917			
	13/-/-		A shelter for the men where needed, were repaired with a certain amount of newly-fitted trench clothes and recovered.	

WAR DIARY
INTELLIGENCE SUMMARY.
(Erase heading not required.)

Army Form C. 2118.

Place	Date	Hour	Summary of Events and Information	Remarks and references to Appendices
[illegible]	[illegible] Aug 1917		carried out every morning by men of the Battalion parties were found subject to some of the Battalion	
Neuve Eglise Red Farm	23rd Aug 1917 to 24th Aug 1917		BRIGADE RESERVE — to the Battalion was employed in the following work. The truck in front of Red Farm trenches. Improved. Parties were supplied to clear jumped off trenches away from [illegible] Road [illegible] to 14 HRS. [illegible] to 14 HRS. Baths — hrs — Close Order Drill. Red (Special Parade)	
	25th Aug		Musketry Test — Bayonet on scratch — 277 Lewis Gun instruction.	
	26th Aug		Bren shown of Musketry Test. Close Order Drill — Gas Drill — Rifle Exercises.	

Army Form C. 2118.

WAR DIARY
or
INTELLIGENCE SUMMARY.
(Erase heading not required.)

Instructions regarding War Diaries and Intelligence Summaries are contained in F.S. Regs., Part II. and the Staff Manual respectively. Title pages will be prepared in manuscript.

9

Place	Date	Hour	Summary of Events and Information	Remarks and references to Appendices
Trenches 27th Aug	27th Aug 1917		7th Aug — Glorious Hot & Hot – Company Drill – Company Drill – Sig Drill. (Lecture on Infantry used patrol formation.)	
Gomiecourt 27.8.17 to 30			Had the Trenches Bermens boundary to Torrier's Quarry 7·3+ 2 O sections. At 6 p.m. orders were issued to each Battalion affected to sidi. Dispositions on taking over lines — D Company — Right front company A — Left front company B — Right support company Hdq & I, & 2 Platoon — Kitchen Crater Close Support CHESHIRE QUARRY. 1 Platoon — Local Support, McVey Street	

WAR DIARY
INTELLIGENCE SUMMARY

Army Form C. 2118.

Place	Date	Hour	Summary of Events and Information	Remarks and references to Appendices
Trenches Loos No 10	27th Aug to 31st Aug 1917		"C" Company — Left Support Company. Coy. HQ & 1½ platoons — Reserve Line R>6d. ½ platoon — Local Support. A slight increase in artillery activity than during previous tour. Enemy very alert at night and his Machine Guns very active. No enemy patrols encountered or seen. The inclement weather made a great deal of trench-mat work necessary. The wire at several points was strengthened and new rows put out. The several wire patrols patrolled in front of our wire each night and small french patrols maintained touch with Battalions on right and left, and between Companies. At 4.30 a.m. on the 31st inst. enemy put down a very heavy barrage of trench Mortars, immediately followed by our artillery Barrage, as equally intense Area shelled — A 34.a 8 8 to Turner's Quarry. The garrisons in the Advanced Front Line were withdrawn and our Machine guns and artillery opened fire. Bombing Parties were organised and as soon	GUN SUPPORT

WAR DIARY
INTELLIGENCE SUMMARY
(Erase heading not required.)

Army Form C. 2118.

Place	Date	Hour	Summary of Events and Information	Remarks and references to Appendices
Somme/près Ribecourt	27th Aug 1917		As the barrage lifted men of our Scouts bombing parties worked towards Turner's Quarry. No enemy were encountered but traces of recently deserted positions of our trench just North of Turner's Quarry. The enemy under cover of the barrage had apparently retired just North of Turner's Quarry and bombed eastwards for about 100 yards and then retired. Considerable damage was done to the trenches and wire. Astrong Lewis Gun Barry was set at night repairing the damage.	

Crowning
Lieut-Colonel
13th (S) Bn Yorks Regt

WAR DIARY
or
INTELLIGENCE SUMMARY.

(Erase heading not required.)

Army Form C. 2118.

Vol 16

Confidential.

War Diary
-of-
13th. (S) Battn. Yorkshire Regiment

From 1st. September 1917
to 30th. September 1917.

(Volume 16).

Army Form C. 2118.

WAR DIARY
or
INTELLIGENCE SUMMARY
(Erase heading not required.)

Instructions regarding War Diaries and Intelligence Summaries are contained in F. S. Regs., Part II. and the Staff Manual respectively. Title pages will be prepared in manuscript.

Place	Date	Hour	Summary of Events and Information	Remarks and references to Appendices
Ext. 51. Guillemont Trench No 16	1st to 4th Sept 1917		(On the Trenches Left Sub-Sector of Brigade Front) Gun Alarms, etc. 7.9/2/1st inclusive to Turners Quarry. 7.34 b. 10. 0 exclusive. During the latter part of the tour the clear moonlight nights were a great hindrance to our patrols who were repeatedly fired upon in endeavouring to reconnoitre enemy wire. a. Moon eclipse on enemy trenches at 7.89.a. planned for night of Sept 3rd/4th 1917 had to be postponed until night of 4th/5th Sept 1917, owing to the moon. The artillery first reconnoitred nightly on enemy trenches. Sniping on our own front was fairly active at night. During the whole tour the Battalion only sustained one casualty.	
Cross Roads at Cemetery Road x 2 c 30 10 8 t	4th Sept to 8th Sept		On the night of the 4th/5th September, the 10th Battalion Stafford Regiment took over the left sub-sector of the Brigade front. On relief the Battalion proceeded into Brigade Support, taking over the dispositions as my previous tour. "A", "B", "C" on improved accommodation at 4 Support Boulevard had been slightly improved on by 10th Battalion in their spare time, but greatly interest was the previous occupation of the position. During the present several old unimproved shelters have fitted down and accommodation of large reports shelters dug out the Trust (late) Battalions were started but weather prevented its mightly. "D" Company proceeded to the line on the 5th/6th September	

WAR DIARY
or
INTELLIGENCE SUMMARY.
(Erase heading not required.)

Army Form C. 2118.

Place	Date	Hour	Summary of Events and Information	Remarks and references to Appendices
Croisilles Sector Road 84 X.2.8.80.10.	14/6	8pm	to carry out the Minor Enterprise on enemy trenches in T.19.c. It was proposed to cut two gaps, by wire cutters, in the outer belt between T.19.a.0.05.80 and T.19.c.0.10.25. After the successful accomplishment of this task two parties were to be blown, by bangalore torpedoes, in the inner belt. If possible the enterprise was to be carried out without Artillery co-operation, but if so pre-arranged code word to be sent if necessary. Objects:— (1) To obtain identifications. (2) To capture enemy machine gun. (3) to destroy emplacements. Lieut. B.H. Thompson was in command of the Enterprise. Parties, which was constituted as follows:— (a) Second Lieutenant E.J. Rawlings and 18 other ranks were to enter the night gap and push forward to trench 226 burning approach of trench near exit, to obtain trench, one as a stopping party, the other working up the gun, the other party would work along trench eastwards towards suspected dug-out and Jewbow Lieutenant Rawlings with 3 other ranks + additional would act eastwards along trench, and bombers P. Drake were to be carried by this party for destroying dug outs. (b) Second Lieutenant A.E. Shorthouse and 13 other ranks were to enter

Army Form C. 2118.

WAR DIARY
or
INTELLIGENCE SUMMARY.
(Erase heading not required.)

Place	Date	Hour	Summary of Events and Information	Remarks and references to Appendices
Cross Roads Cemetery Road	4th to 8th Sept.		left gaps and reach forward to trench. A bombing squad of 9 men would form a blocking party facing Westerdeb. Two men to work along trench Eastwards towards Sabr. On arriving at sap I then would mount up the sides operated by Second Lieutenant Northcote and 3 men working along parapet and parados. (c) Lieut. J. E. Simpton and 10 other ranks with Lewis Gun would form the support and covering party. (d) Second Lieutenant P. R. Thompson, Sgt. Parley, 2 Lewis Guns and teams would form the Left Flank Protection. (e) Corporal A. Robson and six scouts would watch the Right Flank to prevent surprise. (f) Party of 1 N.C.O. and 4 men, R.Es to fire the Bangalore Torpedoes. A forward Company Head Quarters was established in front of our wire, also a telephone station, whilst Right Advanced Battalion Head Quarters at Cheshire Quarry in close touch with the Raiding Parties. The parties left our lines at 9 p.m. The enemy were very much on the alert and on approaching Noside were our parties were met by	

Army Form C. 2118.

WAR DIARY
or
INTELLIGENCE SUMMARY.
(Erase heading not required.)

Place	Date	Hour	Summary of Events and Information	Remarks and references to Appendices
Gross Post Cemetery Road.	17th to 8th Sept.		Heavy Machine Gun and riffe fire and had to withdraw. A second attempt made when all was quiet met with heavy fire and the raid had to be abandoned.	
Vaucellette Farm to X.13.c.3.5.	19th to 21st Sept.		Brigade Reserve:- On returning from the Minor Enterprise "D" Company had only Breakfast at Vaucellette Farm before proceeding to their billets at Heudicourt. During the period in Brigade Reserve baths are placed at the disposal of the Battalion and clean underclothing distributed. The tactical method of training as on previous Tours was carried out.	
Trenches P.26.d. H.U. 80.	19th to 23rd Sept.		In the Trenches - (Left sub-sector of Brigade Front - Gin Ave. T.9/a/7.4. exclusive to Turner's Quarry, T.34.b.10.0 inclusive). The enemy was very active at night. Intermittently throughout the night the bombed his wire and front Rifle Grenades and Light T.M.S in front of our ridges. Patrols were sent out nightly to examine and if possible to get enemy wire not wire cutters. Owing to the alertness of the enemy this was not possible. Comparatively the enemy Artillery activity was not so active as during the previous Tour. No	

WAR DIARY or INTELLIGENCE SUMMARY

Army Form C. 2118.

Place	Date	Hour	Summary of Events and Information	Remarks and references to Appendices
Gommecourt Wood	1st to 2nd Sept		enemy was entrenched beyond the cemetery. Each dugout was in the improvement of trenches, especially on the support & reserve and Gun Support on the lift of the Battalion Front. Sundays were not clearly cut, gas masks. Casualties during tour – 3 other ranks.	
Cross Post Cemetery Wood	3rd to 7th Sept		Brigade Support. Battalion again carried the dugouts. Working Parties supplied daily to the district from to continue the work for deepening and new front line trenches, to Gun Support and the usual carrying parties were found at night for the Front Line Battalion. Most of the old entrenched shelters of the previous trenches are demolished and new ones erected. On the night of the 7th inst, the 12th Battalion Suffolk Regt. was ordered to co-operate and moved to their lines if necessary. This was not found necessary.	

Army Form C. 2118.

WAR DIARY
or
INTELLIGENCE SUMMARY.

(Erase heading not required.)

Instructions regarding War Diaries and Intelligence
Summaries are contained in F. S. Regs., Part II.
and the Staff Manual respectively. Title pages
will be prepared in manuscript.

Place	Date	Hour	Summary of Events and Information	Remarks and references to Appendices
Vaucellette Farm. K.13.c.5.3	27th to 30th Sept.		Brigade Reserve.- Until Nov. had applications were enquired by the Brigade and Lewis Gunners Sergeant Armourer inspected the rifles and Lewis Guns. On the 29th and the Transporting Officer inspected all transport at work; also the Regimental Transport. Regimental sports were held at Vaucellette Farm on the 29th instant. There was a large number of entries and some good racing was witnessed. Several of the events caused a great deal of amusement. Programmes of sports is attached. Tournaments were also held. Lieutenant Colonel B.G. Buxton distributed the prizes to the successful competitors.	

D.S.Blakely Lieut-Colonel,
Commanding 10th (S) Bn. Yorkshire Regiment

WAR DIARY
or
INTELLIGENCE SUMMARY.
(Erase heading not required.)

Army Form C. 2118.

Place	Date	Hour	Summary of Events and Information	Remarks and references to Appendices
			10th (Service) Battalion Yorkshire Regiment	
			Programme of Sports	
			to be held on Third Ypres, Vauxhall Farm on 19th September 1917.	
			President: Lieut-Colonel B.L. Raper	
			Judges: Capt R.A. Bigg-Wither, Capt W Pearson, RAMC, Capt J R A Boyle, Lieut R S Thompson	
			Starter: Regt Sgt-Major G Hodges	
			Events	
			1. 100 yards Flat Race 6. Ambling Band Race	
			2. Three legged Race 7. Obstacle Race	
			3. 220 yards Flat Race 8. Relay Relief in Pairs	
			4. Boot Race (Twenty pairs a-side) 9. Bayonet Wheelbarrow Race	
			5. Relay Race – Teams of 4 men 10. Runners Walking Race	
			All entries will be taken to the field of the Orderly Room before which will be adjudged later.	
			Prizes will be awarded. God Save The King	

Army Form C. 2118

WAR DIARY
or
INTELLIGENCE SUMMARY
(Erase heading not required.)

Instructions regarding War Diaries and Intelligence Summaries are contained in F. S. Regs., Part II. and the Staff Manual respectively. Title Pages will be prepared in manuscript.

Vol 17

CONFIDENTIAL

War Diary
of
13th (Service) Battalion Yorkshire Regt.

From 1st. October 1917.
to
31st. October 1917.

Place	Date	Hour	Summary of Events and Information	Remarks and references to Appendices

WAR DIARY or INTELLIGENCE SUMMARY

Army Form C. 2118

Place	Date	Hour	Summary of Events and Information	Remarks and references to Appendices
Ref map 1/S.E. Scale 20,000 BONNELIEU R.26.d. 10.50	1st Oct 1917 to 8th Oct 1917		In the trenches. (Left Sub-sector of Brigade fronts:- GIN AVENUE R.29.a.7.1. inclusive to TURNER'S QUARRY R.34.6.10.0. exclusive) The dark nights considerably facilitated the reconnoitering of the enemy wire by our nightly patrols. The raid by the 2/R. Suffolk Regiment had apparently had a quietening effect on the enemy. His M.G. fire had greatly diminished & his activity generally during the early stages of the tour was at a minimum. There was almost immediately noticed the whole tour and in consequence a larger amount of hard work was essential and falls required constant attention. During the previous tour, on the night of 18/19th September 1917, No 24657 Private (A. Harrison) and No. 42243 Private J. H. Price formed part of a patrol. When the patrol was within 20 yards of the enemy wire it came under heavy fire and Lance Corporal Carter was mortally wounded. Under heavy fire, keeping through a barrage of rifle grenades near the Harrison & Price assisted L/C Carter and carried him to our lines. The Commanding Officer had recommended the above men for the award of the MILITARY MEDAL & the announcement granting the award appeared in Divisional Routine Orders No 29991 Private L.C. Toakley had been recommended for the award of the DISTINGUISHED CONDUCT MEDAL M180th and his name appears in this award on Divisional Routine Orders, dated 3.10.'17, for the following act of gallantry: On the afternoon of 9th September 1917, Ft. Handley challenged great courage and initiative in rendering assistance to the pilot	

WAR DIARY
INTELLIGENCE SUMMARY
(Erase heading not required.)

Army Form C. 2118

Place	Date	Hour	Summary of Events and Information	Remarks and references to Appendices
Ref. Map 57c S.E. Scale 20,000 GONNELIEU R.36.d. 20 to 30	1st Oct. 1917 to 6th Oct. 1917		and observed two of our aeroplanes which came down on fire about 500 yards behind our front line trenches. Also he secured valuable material from the Flaming machine. During the night of the 1st/2nd instant an enemy patrol was observed to retire along the whole of the front and the enemy artillery was particularly active along the whole of the front and the village of GONNELIEU which seemed a great deal of attention. The enemy intermittent shelling indicated an impending heid but nothing materialised. Our casualties were 3 killed & 6 wounded, two of whom remained at duty. One of the tanks proceeding on patrol or reconnoitring work on the night of 5/6th returned with a left wheel of tank No. 2679 Female. It was made forward through the enemy front line helped by a machine gun bullet. On leaving this N.C.O. brought him and 200 yards under heavy fire. For his gallant action he was awarded the Military Medal. The 1st and 2nd Regiment of Ghurkas on our left was ordered to raid the enemy trenches in R.15 on night of 5/6th October 1917. In co-operation with this enterprise a smoke barrage to deceive the enemy was discharged from our Advanced Frontline between this BANTEUX and SONNET Ronds. "A" Company performed this operation. Practically no retaliation took place on our front as a result of this remote barrage. On the 5th & 6th October the enemy artillery was more active and appeared to be registering D. Mills Alley, Hud Alley and our front & Support lines in IP. 29.d. R. 33.a preparatory to an

WAR DIARY or INTELLIGENCE SUMMARY

Army Form C. 2118

Place	Date	Hour	Summary of Events and Information	Remarks and references to Appendices
Hut Railton W.16.c.	9th.		road. Operation orders were issued to take effect in this event & special vigilance was kept up by means of snipers listening posts & patrols. No action, however, by the evening followed. Orders were received that the 10th Division in Artillery, Pioneer Battalion, and two Field Coys. R.E. would be relieved between 5th & 10th October, by the 20th Division. The 61st Infantry Brigade relieved the 31st Infantry Brigade on the night October 5th. 7th Battn. Duke of Cornwall's L.I. relieving the Battalion. On relief the Battalion was taken to Billets at the Hub Railton W.16.c. by Dearville Railway and after spending the night there on the following afternoon again entrained by Decauville to Peronne. The Regimental Transport together with the transport of the other units in the Brigade, also proceeded to Peronne by road on the same day.	
Peronne	10th.		Peronne was left the following morning, the Battalion entraining at Peronne - Flamincourt Station at 8.45 a.m. Saulmotes to Puchevillers (?) the detraining station was reached at 12.45 p.m. and after a little road march the Battalion arrived at Bailey the allotted Billeting Area. No transport by Regimental Transport Moved by road Journey to Bailey he remembers proceeding by road was Peronne to bel 11th instant the orders of O.C. No 4 Coy. Divisional Train.	
Bailey 51c.Y.p.d.too			The day afternoon at Bailey was spent in cleaning up generally for the 13th instant. Training areas were allotted to Coys. to carry on in accordance with Brigade nemo drawn up by the C.O. Corps commenced Football, Mulets, Boxing Competitions.	

WAR DIARY
INTELLIGENCE SUMMARY

Place	Date	Hour	Summary of Events and Information	Remarks and references to Appendices
Bus. le Leger	Oct 29 to 31st		Concerts and every form of amusement were organised by the Battalion Sports Committee and every endeavour was made to afford relaxation to the men. Divisional Brigade Competitions in Football, Boxing &c. took place & efforts were given by Troupes from the 13th D.A. & to the Divisional respectively. Two recent internals of Lieut-Col. G.H. Long, 5th Suffolk Regiment, was attached for duty with the Battalion, and joined on the 15th instant, and on Major J Jingo the 2nd in Command being appointed to the Command of the Divisional Depot Battalion, Lieut Col Long assumed the duties of 2nd in Command of the Battalion. Major General & Inconby C.M.G. D.S.O. Commanding the Division, inspected the Brigade on parade on the 21st instant, and decorated the Officers, N.C.O's & men with the ribbons of the medals awarded them for their recent gallantry in action. On the 26th & 29th October the 121st Infantry Brigade carried out a practice attack, the objective being the Wood in V.20, 26 & V.27 in accordance with training instructions issued. The Barrages were demonstrated by flags & each Battalion allotted definite objectives. Owing however, to inoculation the Battalion was not in full strength on either occasion. WARLUS & .... and Warlincourt Abbey nor cdt to .... 75th Brigade Group on the 29th October, the Battalion being attached 113 Bdes.	

K.H.E. D.H. Lieut-Col.
Comdg. 13th (S) Bn Rifle Brigade
attd 113 Bde. in Lieu A. Legen.

WAR DIARY
or
INTELLIGENCE SUMMARY.

Army Form C. 2118.

CONFIDENTIAL

War Diary of
1st (Garrison) Bn. Yorkshire Regiment
From 1st November 1917
To 30th June 1918
(Volume 12)

WAR DIARY / INTELLIGENCE SUMMARY

Army Form C. 2118.

Place	Date	Hour	Summary of Events and Information	Remarks and references to Appendices
SUS St LEGER	1st Apl 1917 to 16th Apl 1917		Training areas around SUS St LEGER were allotted to the Battalion and the following scheme of training was carried out:— 1 Group in support for attack from around position — should front line troops achieve & carry an advanced trench capturing the strongpoint or breaker for attack on a village, be [?] Specialist training — Lewis Gun, Bombing and Kevin Gun. Rifle and Lewis Gun firing Practice were carried out on the Ranges in the Battalion and Brigade Field Days were held on the 6th inst, a Brigade Ophanon? being carried out showing around the SUS St LEGER— BOUQUEMAISON Area. The usual Reserve training, together with Boxing, Competitions and Sports Meeting, Football although without drive for the men and all ranks etc.	

Army Form C. 2118.

WAR DIARY
or
INTELLIGENCE SUMMARY.
(Erase heading not required.)

Instructions regarding War Diaries and Intelligence Summaries are contained in F. S. Regs., Part II. and the Staff Manual respectively. Title pages will be prepared in manuscript.

Place	Date	Hour	Summary of Events and Information	Remarks and references to Appendices
BARLY 57c 4/10 000	16th Nov 1917		The 16th November the Battalion moved by route march to BARLY, occupying the allotted accommodation in the village.	
ACHIET-LE-PETIT 57c 4/10 000	17th Nov		The Battalion remained at BARLY.	
	18th Nov 1917		The Battalion moved from BARLY at 5A m on the 18th and proceeded by road march to the camp at ACHIET-LE-PETIT, arriving at 11.30 A.m. The 1st Battalion Grenadier Guards took over the camp on the 19th November, the Battalion having to reconnoitre at ROCQUIGNY via ACHIET-LE-GRAND – BIHUCOURT – BIEFVILLERS – BAPAUME and LE TRANSLOY.	
ROCQUIGNY 57c 4/10 000	19th Nov 1917		From 10 A.m. on the 19th November the Battalion was held in readiness to move at an hour's notice. "C" Company moved to the BEAUMETZ area on the afternoon of the 20th inst. No operations recommenced preparatory to the Battalion	

Army Form C. 2118.

WAR DIARY
or
INTELLIGENCE SUMMARY.
(Erase heading not required.)

Instructions regarding War Diaries and Intelligence Summaries are contained in F. S. Regs., Part II. and the Staff Manual respectively. Title pages will be prepared in manuscript.

Place	Date	Hour	Summary of Events and Information	Remarks and references to Appendices
HERMIES K.12.d.00.00	17th Nov 1917		Nothing of interest. The Battalion moved to the encampment in the trenches at about 11 PM.	
BENNETZ Les-Cambrai 57.d.4.00.00	20th Nov 1917		The following day the Battalion moved into the relieving the 5th York & Lanc Regiment. The 11th Durhams moved up to make preparations to attack BOURLON WOOD and VILLAGE on 23rd November 1917. The 51st Division were ordered to attack FONTAINE NOTRE DAME on the Right. The 36th Division was ordered to attack QUARRY WOOD and INCHY on the Left. The attack was carried out by 119th Infantry Brigade and 121st Infantry Brigade. The 120th Infantry Brigade was in Divisional Reserve in the trench system S.W. of GRAINCOURT. Boundaries:- On the Right 119th Infantry Brigade - Cross-Roads E.34.a & E.16.d J.6. Then northwards by 119th Brigade - E.16.d J.6. Then	

WAR DIARY or INTELLIGENCE SUMMARY

Army Form C. 2118.

Place	Date	Hour	Summary of Events and Information	Remarks and references to Appendices
SUGAR FACTORY E.29.a HUDDIVEDS	22nd Nov 1917		E.12.d.1.1. to point of junction E.12.c.6.199. The I.L.L. has to push forward with the railway at E.12.c.7.8. moved to Infantry Brigade. (1) 1st Brigade of 36th Division on our left. 99.00 at 2 on DELIGHT MILL E.18.a.8.2 inclusive. (c) Rhine – Burman – Rose Junction E.14. – Road Junction E.12.c.07.20 – CROSS ROADS E.12.c.4.9. – CHURCH Junction of track and railway in E.16.1. all inclusive to 1st Division. The 10th Battalion McAllan Regiment on the right and the 13th Battalion Yorkshire Regiment on the left carried out the failure. 1. A' Zero the Battalion moved in Colonel B by Battalion commanding 13th Battalion Yorkshire Regiment on the morning of the noble. 2. The attack was failed & Zombra Traverse was today these had from the Saxony.	

Army Form C. 2118.

WAR DIARY
or
INTELLIGENCE SUMMARY.
(Erase heading not required.)

Instructions regarding War Diaries and Intelligence Summaries are contained in F. S. Regs., Part II. and the Staff Manual respectively. Title pages will be prepared in manuscript.

Place	Date	Hour	Summary of Events and Information	Remarks and references to Appendices
SUGAR FACTORY E.9.q. NIEUPORT trench system 9.0.p.v.w.x			*[faded handwritten entries]*	
			NIEUPORT	
		9	Bn rested. Coys kept in readiness to move at short notice to reinforce the Infantry trenches which it appeared had that time was to no doing.	
		10	FACTORY intention tend was to reinforce and east to SUGAR FACTORY.	
		11	SUGAR FACTORY in E.9.9 with first Platoon Hd Quarters will remain at the SUGAR FACTORY been formed, when it will move to Trench Road E.9.c. 30.40	
		12	Recconaissance Road SUGAR FACTORY	
		13	10.30 a.m.	
			The advance of the Infantry and Tanks was supported by a Barrage — Shrapnel H.E. and Shrapnel Barrage fell down from F.30 — N.1 along the South edge of the WOOD, taken along the front between F.30 & N.30 further East to the Barrage lifted 300 yards every 10 minutes after the first lift at Zero.	

WAR DIARY

INTELLIGENCE SUMMARY

(Erase heading not required.)

Army Form C. 2118.

Place	Date	Hour	Summary of Events and Information	Remarks and references to Appendices

SUGAR FACTORY E.29 a. MOEUVRES	2nd Nov 1917 to 3rd Nov 1917		3. The attack will be made in four waves.
			 (a) 1st + 2nd waves. R Coy D Company
			                                           R. [Regt.] C Company
			 (b) 3rd and 4th waves. R [Regt.] B Company
			                                           R [Regt.] A Company = 178
			 4. First objective – trench beyond —
			 Second objective – village of BOURLON.
			 5. On reaching 2nd objective from K.9.b. troops will consolidate on a line roughly N. end of village in E.6.d. to QUARRY in E.7.a.7. – E.11.b.
			 6. "A" Company will, after 2nd objective is reached, take up a support position about CITADEL E.11.b.
			 "B" Company in reserve position at about E.11.b.2.10.
			 BOUNDARIES — On Right M Regt – touch maintained at E.1.d.1.1.
			 Wally through Mourling — E.9.d.8. junction of trench & railway — E.6.b. — M.1.a.1 — E.3.a.1 – 90.00.
			 to 1st Canal.
			 On Left – 10th Brown & Wales Regt, in touch with Regt. OK R. [Regt.] on Regt. – right	

WAR DIARY
or
INTELLIGENCE SUMMARY.
(Erase heading not required.)

Army Form C. 2118.

Place	Date	Hour	Summary of Events and Information	Remarks and references to Appendices
SUGAR FACTORY E.29.a MOEUVRES (Near West Flers cambrai)	23rd Nov 1917 24th Nov 1917		The attack was met by heavy machine gun and rifle fire. Strong opposition was met with at E.16.b.7.0 and E.9.a.1 whereupon Ken.a.1 were ordered very accurately and with 50 rounds being expended from dug-outs at E.11.c.55.65 at 12.55 a. The village was reached at E.12.c.59 by 12 The attack was open checked at E.12.c.at 1.50 p.m. as my companies were exposed to fire from the flanks which were not occupied by infantry. Shoot from the front of the advance of the troops on the flanks.	
		12.24 p.m.	The Battalion fire burst on a line E.12.c.00.00 — E.16.c.10.00 and got into touch with the 20th Durham Middlesex Regiment on the Right and Passed in a strong front on left with 4 officers and 180 men the trenches were manned by 13th Durham and Coy Regiment as gain the 10th on the Brigade had ordered the SUGAR FACTORY.	
K.16.c.9.1 85th Nov 1917			The Division was relieved on night of 24th/25th November by the 62nd Division. The 121st Infantry Brigade was relieved by the 178th Infantry Brigade.	

Army Form C. 2118.

WAR DIARY
or
INTELLIGENCE SUMMARY.
(Erase heading not required.)

Place	Date	Hour	Summary of Events and Information	Remarks and references to Appendices
K.10 c 9.7.	26th Nov 1917		The Battalion being relieved by the 5th Yorks & Lancs Regiment on relief the Battalion moved to Bihucourt.	
BERTINCOURT	26th Nov 1917		On the 26th November the Battalion proceeded to accommodation at BERTINCOURT, reaching billets about 6 p.m. The following morning moved the 61st Brigade Front turned over at YPRES at 2 p.m. on the morning of the 27th November.	
BELLACOURT L.16 c 9.4 / L.10 c 9.10	27th Nov 1917	12 noon	LE.10.c.9.10 1.2.8.9. The remaining Companies reached at 12 noon, the Battalion being in billets in BELLACOURT.	
			The remainder who covered and supervised equipment relieved Batt. were returned to the Battalion on the 27th Nov. and on the 29th were escorted to the Base. The officers the Battalion should be kept in ignorance to them sent new notes in advance.	

18/12/1917

Lewis — Colonel
6th W. Yorkshire Regiment
Commanding

Army Form C. 2118.

WAR DIARY
or
INTELLIGENCE SUMMARY.
(Erase heading not required.)

CONFIDENTIAL

War Diary
of
13th (Service) Battalion Yorkshire Regiment
From 1st December 1917.
To 31st December 1917.

(Volume 19).

WAR DIARY
or
INTELLIGENCE SUMMARY.

(Erase heading not required.)

Army Form C. 2118.

Place	Date	Hour	Summary of Events and Information	Remarks and references to Appendices
ECOIVRES Ref II Map 1/40,000	1st Dec 1917		The 1/7th Middlesex Batn. Brigaded with the 1/8th and 1/9th Battalions completed their training & marched to billets at the VILLE, Huts B2 & B6, near St YBERT and from ECOIVRES being the relieving unit. At 10th December 1917, the 1/7th MIDDLESEX reconnoitred on RECANT OOMP being billeted in the Battalion.	
ECOIVRES 51st Divn	4th		On arriving in the area the 1/7th Middlesex Infantry Brigade were in Divisional Reserve to the 1st Division.	
I.35 d.5.8 BULLECOURT MAP	8th Dec	9h 10h	Kept the 8th 9th 10th Relieving the Relieved the 1/1st Infantry Brigade and 2nd Battalion Royal Worcestershire Regt on the Relieved 2/2nd Battalion Royal Worcestershire Sector in the Sector— Dispositions:— Battalion Head Quarters — I.17 a.5.9 B and D Coys — Support Coy at I.13 a. B Coy — Front Line a. C Coy T. 29 a. D Coy 11 a. During the tour in support the Companies working parties and Patrols were found daily for duty in the support villages of ECOUST and reconnaissance and repair of defences and practising and defence of line, and from the Brigade.	
	9th Dec		During the 1st, 2nd, 8th, 9th, and 10th Dec. At 5.00 am on the 9th Dec the Battalion took over a Battalion front and Brigade Sector as a Battalion front and Sector the relieving units on the 9th December being the 1/5th K.S.L.I. Regt and 10th Bn. Middlesex Regt on relieved	

Army Form C. 2118.

WAR DIARY
INTELLIGENCE SUMMARY
(Erase heading not required.)

Instructions regarding War Diaries and Intelligence Summaries are contained in F.S. Regs., Part II. and the Staff Manual respectively. Title pages will be prepared in manuscript.

Place	Date	Hour	Summary of Events and Information	Remarks and references to Appendices
TRCHS IN FRONT OF BULLECOURT MAP 1/10,000	9th Dec to 9th Dec 1917		their fronts, thus relieving the 91st Bon Middlesex (right coy. on completion of relief) moved to Brigade support on the left, the Battalion occupying the support position on the night. This new disposition was completed by 4 p.m. New disposition of Coys:- "A" Coy. – in Battalion Reserve to the right sub-sector in LINCOLN SUPPORT and BURG TRENCH "B" Coy. – Sunken Road, T.17.d and 18.c. "C" & "D" Coys. – Sunken Roads, T.23.d, 29.b. until 30.a. The Brigade were relieved from the line on the 10th December by the 180th Infantry Brigade. On relief the Battalion proceeded to billets	
ECOUST ST. MEIN	10th Dec 1917 to 11th Dec		at BELFAST CAMP, ECOUST. The following is an extract from 91st Infantry Brigade Operation Order received on arrival in Divisional Reserve:– "There have been indications of abnormal enemy movement on this front, viz:- columns of infantry, 3,000 others, marching through enemy back areas, also considerable columns of artillery and cavalry moving north. There has been abnormal aeroplane activity on Corps front, and a letter captured on a prisoner refers to an intensified offensive on a big scale by the enemy. It is thought that the enemy may attempt a surprise attack on a big scale in this vicinity	

WAR DIARY or INTELLIGENCE SUMMARY

Army Form C. 2118.

Place	Date	Hour	Summary of Events and Information	Remarks and references to Appendices
	17th Dec		Shortly read until further orders the Brigade will:— (a) Stand to from 6.35 a.m. to 6.45 a.m. (b) Be prepared to move at 5 minutes notice from 6.45 a.m. to 7.30 a.m. (c) Be prepared to move at half an hour's notice for the remainder of the day and at night. On receipt of orders No. 4045 from Brigade Head Quarters. (a) Moved into bivouac to have breakfast, but not having Field Kitchens and Cook Arrangements will occupy the days allowed thus as follows:— 13th Yorkshires (Capt. — from B 10.1.9.3 (exclusive) to SENSEE RIVER (inclusive). At 1 a.m. on the 19th December the order to MOVE was received. Coys were sent after attacked positions in the Capt. Second Lines by 7.45 a.m. Orders to return to camp were received at 8.00 a.m. The enemy had attempted an attack on our right and a fight to send over bombs. Prisoners taken by the attack stated that the 13th Battalion of the Regiment had been ordered on 18th December for the night (sic) of this attack. Any other details that this were was to be confirmed by Divisional troops.	

WAR DIARY or INTELLIGENCE SUMMARY

Army Form C. 2118.

Place	Date	Hour	Summary of Events and Information	Remarks and references to Appendices
ERWILLERS	10th Dec to 17th Dec 1917		In consequence of this information Units were ordered to take up positions in Corps Second line by 5.30 a.m. on 15th December. No attack, however, developed and Battalions were ordered back to camp/or. The Corps Second line was again occupied on the following morning and during the afternoon stood to and stood on account of a S.O.S. message being received from East Pendriox. This state of readiness was maintained until the 17th December when the above operation Order was cancelled. The Battalion was ordered to relieve the 11th Bn. East Yorkshire Light Infantry in the line on 18th December 1917.	
LINCOLN SUPPORT	18th Dec to 23rd Dec 1917		(See Maps Tourpé - Right 1st sector of Brigade Front - Gouzeaucourt - 1 w a 6.3 to J.7.b.5.9.) The trenches taken over were in a fair condition except the various front line communication trenches were considerably. The gunpit telamen and was our approaches and putted with shell holes but necessitating work was greatly hampered by fog. Drilling on both sides went during the last days particularly on the 19th, 20th at night. Visibility during the day was very poor and by the Tourpé front was constantly strengthened. Many of the known enemy positions were located and wire was constantly strengthened. Strong enemy working parties, at night, were observed and were much occasional. Lewis patrols, information of and mission was sent to Battalion Head Quarters dealt instilling and machine gun fire effectively dispersed the parties. Very few casualties were sustained during the tour.	

Army Form C. 2118.

WAR DIARY
or
INTELLIGENCE SUMMARY.
(Erase heading not required.)

Instructions regarding War Diaries and Intelligence Summaries are contained in F.S. Regs., Part II. and the Staff Manual respectively. Title pages will be prepared in manuscript.

Place	Date	Hour	Summary of Events and Information	Remarks and references to Appendices
FRANKLEIGH CAMP	24th Dec to 26th Dec 1917		On relief by the 11th Bn Argyll & Sutherland Highlanders the Battalion moved to Divisional Reserve at BELFAST CAMP. Billets were allotted to the Battalion on Christmas Day. On the following day a Christmas dinner was served to the troops comprising:— Roast Beef, Roast Potatoes and Plum Pudding. Rations and Rum were issued and apples, oranges nuts &c. Dessert. Beer and Stout. The Commanding officer and Second in command visited the men partaking of their meal and hearty toasts were interchanged. Competitive sports were organised in the evening.	
	27th to 31st Dec 1918		The 40th Division was relieved to extend their front on the night of the 5th December 1917 to the south and took over the front held by 2nd Division.	

A5834 Wt. W4973/M687 750,000 8/16 D. D. & L. Ltd. Form/C.2118/13.

WAR DIARY or INTELLIGENCE SUMMARY

Army Form C. 2118.

Place	Date	Hour	Summary of Events and Information	Remarks and references to Appendices
U.96.c.31 Ref 51.L.S.E N.W Sh 57.000	9/11 to N.W Dec 1917		Relieve to this order the 91st Infantry Brigade relieved the 70th Infantry Brigade on the left sub sector The Division and 8/9/8th November. The Battalion relieved the 10th Bn Royal Welsh Fusiliers as support in the following sectors - Battalion Head Quarters - U.96.c.31. "A" Coy - U.96.c and d "B" Coy - In reserve to Regt and action J.08.c and 6.d.b "C" Coy - Regt moving S.E and N.W in 0.3.d. "D" Coy - Factory Post U.96.c. Owing to the enemys recent attack on this front every precaution was taken - all troops standing to from 6.h on to 6.30 a.m. daily. The usual working parties supplied by the Support Batln went out nightly. In accordance with relief table issued by Brigade the Battalion relieved the 14th Bn Suffolk Regt on the Dec 6th 51st Division. Donrady 13th (S) Bn Yorkshire Regiment	

Army Form C. 2118.

WAR DIARY
or
INTELLIGENCE SUMMARY.
(Erase heading not required.)

CONFIDENTIAL

WAR DIARY
of
13th (Service) Battalion Yorkshire Regiment

From 1st January 1918
To 31st January 1918

(Volume 20).

WAR DIARY
INTELLIGENCE SUMMARY

Army Form C. 2118.

Place	Date	Hour	Summary of Events and Information	Remarks and references to Appendices
U.28.c.9.5. Ref. Map Arras Sheet. U.1.6.C.6 Scale 1/10,000	1st January 1918 to 4th January		In the trenches - Right sub-sector of the Brigade front Boundaries:- Right - U.29.c.25.90 to U.22.c.50.45 left). The atmospheric conditions were very keen, sharp frosts at night and falls of snow during the day at frequent intervals, at times in regular blizzards. Enemy Artillery was very active during the tour, especially on TANK SUPPORT, TANK AVENUE, LONDON RESERVE and LONDON SUPPORT and vicinity of Dah on U.23.c. RAILWAY RESERVE was also shelled intermittently. Our Artillery carried out retaliation shoots. The enemy, however, still continued systematic 'strafs' but no infantry actions developed. Hot food for the men could not be prepared on the line. Hot meals were, therefore, improved under Battalion arrangements in RAILWAY RESERVE and conveyed in food containers to the front line posts by carrying parties. Lieut-Colonel D.J. Baker proceeded on leave of absence on the 3rd January. Major E.B. King taking over command of the Battalion.	
			The 12th Battalion Suffolk Regiment took over the sub-sector on the 4th January and the Battalion, on relief, proceeded to Brigade Reserve in MORY.	
L'ABBAYE, MORY	5th to 8th Jany 1918		Here, baths were allotted and the necessary re-equipping of articles and clothing lost or rendered unserviceable were issued. At 6.30 p.m. on the 8th a S.O.S. message was received from Brigade Head Quarters. The enemy had launched an attack on the Right Company of the Right Sub-sector and were reported in strength on front line between LONDON SUPPORT and old front line and on TANK SUPPORT. Three Companies of 21st Middlesex Regt.	

WAR DIARY
INTELLIGENCE SUMMARY.

(Erase heading not required.)

Army Form C. 2118.

Place	Date	Hour	Summary of Events and Information	Remarks and references to Appendices
L'ABBAYE MORY	5th Jan to 8th Jan 1918		The Battalion in Support, were at one placed at the disposal of O.C. Right Sub-sector, and "A" Coy of 13th Bn. York R. were ordered to move from MORY to neighbourhood of Alabaster Bn. H.Q. came under orders of O.C. Support Bn. "B" Coy was also detailed to move forward and occupy the Intermediate line with its right on BULLECOURT AVENUE. This Company was also under the orders of the O.C. Support Battalion. In the counter-attack the enemy were repulsed from our positions. No Companies of this Battalion actually came to grips with the foe. 17 prisoners were captured in this operation.	
U.28.c.9.8. Ref. Map. Sheet 16 U.1. to C.6 Scale 1/10.000	8th Jan to 12th Jan 1918		In the trenches :- (Right Sub-sector) of the Brigade Front. Boundaries as on previous tour) Enemy Artillery activity had subsided somewhat after the attack on our positions. The usual patrolling activity and reconnaissance work was carried out. He were around the Bhn heads in U.23.c. was usual. N.C. activity strengthened, also at various points along the line. The usual N.C. activity at night towards the latter end of the tour the show set in.	
			Brigade Support :- Dispositions :-	
			Battalion Head Quarters } 1 Company	
			1 Company	
			1 Company	
U.26.c.7.1 Ref. Map. afternoon sheet. Jam U.1. to C.6 Scale 1/10.000	12th Jan to 16th Jan 1918.		1 Company - Railway Embankment, U.26.c.7.1	
			- TIGER TRENCH
			- Sunken Road in C.3.c and C.9.a.
			- Bn. Reserve to Right Sub-sector in RAILWAY RESERVE.

Army Form C. 2118.

WAR DIARY
or
INTELLIGENCE SUMMARY.
(Erase heading not required.)

Place	Date	Hour	Summary of Events and Information	Remarks and references to Appendices
U.28.c.1. Ref. Map from Neuve Chapelle. U.1 to C.6 scale 1/10,000	18th Jan 1918	10th Jan	Carriers were continued daily for transportation to the line and large working parties for work on the line defences proceeded nightly to the front line system. As far as trouble, under the existing conditions the necessary repairs to boots and clothing were rendered. The thaw had thoroughly set in causing falls in trenches and many improvised shelters retain to give. Before proceeding for the next tour of duty on the line, Gum Boots were issued to all troops. It was decided to re-adjust the Brigade frontage in consequence, the Right Sub-sector would be held by two Companies, with one Company in Battalion support, and the remaining Company in Battalion Reserve. The re-adjustment was carried into effect during the tour of the 18th Bn Suffolk R.	3
U.28.c.9.3. Ref. Map from above. U.1 to C.6 scale 1/10,000	16th to 20th Jan 1918		In the trenches - (Boundaries on re-adjustment - Right U.19.a.25.90 Left - U.88.d.00.60) The communication trenches were impracticable owing to the mud and water in consequence of the very rapid thaw, to get to and from the line it was necessary to proceed over the top. Overland duckboard tracks were in course of construction. The work was day standing in the posts on the line maintained, all available labour being concentrated on it. Artillery activity on both sides only rifle-fire. On night of the 18th a raiding party of 1 Officer and 10 other Ranks with bombardier party of 1 N.C.O. and 7 other Ranks left our lines	

WAR DIARY
INTELLIGENCE SUMMARY
(Erase heading not required.)

Army Form C. 2118

Remarks and references to Appendices: **4**

Place	Date	Hour	Summary of Events and Information
U.28.c.9.3 Ref. Map fast Sheet 51b to 57b U.1 to C.6 Scale 1/10,000	19th Jan 1918	16th	at U.22.d.95.45 at 8 p.m. for the purpose of raiding and destroying enemy work in U.22.d.85.60. The enemy work was found unoccupied although there were signs of very recent work. 10 yards of a trench running from the trench under the enemy went was demolished by charges of two stoked Mortar shells. The party then returned to our lines without any casualties. On the 17th the enemy could be plainly seen in full view working on his trenches, which apparently were in a very bad condition. Our men went also on top. The enemy making no attempt to fight. In the afternoon fraternising tactics were attempted by the enemy. Our wire was approached at intervals by batches of the enemy in twos and threes. Eventually two of the enemy came through and were at Dunkery Farm at Dunkers Road. They had no arms or ammunition and were made to put up their hands and enter trench as prisoners. They appeared very hungry.
L'ABBAYE, MORY	20th Jan to 22nd Jan 1918		Brigade Reserve. After the strenuous tour in the line, battling the mud and water, the rest was much appreciated. A great amount of cleaning up was necessary. The erecting of breastworks around huts as a protection against the exploits of hostile aircraft was continued.

WAR DIARY
or
INTELLIGENCE SUMMARY
(Erase heading not required.)

Army Form C. 2118.

Place	Date	Hour	Summary of Events and Information	Remarks and references to Appendices
U.25.c.9.5 Ref Map from Trench Map. U.1 to C.6 Scale 1/10.000	24th to 28th Jan 1918		In the Trenches – Boundaries as on previous tour. The conditions much more favourable than on previous tour. The mud was gradually drying up and several of the C.T.'s had been cleared out. Between the posts and the front line, however, portions of the trench were still impassable. Strong Working Parties found by the Support and Reserve Coys worked nightly at various fronts clearing falls, deepening and widening the trenches and re-laying trench boards.	
U.26.c.1.1 Ref Map from Trench Map. U.1 to C.6 Scale 1/10.000	28th to 31st Jan 1918		Brigade Support. The usual dispositions were occupied. Companies furnished the usual working parties each night and concentrations of wire were made and sent up by trench tramway. The Foot Treatment Centre at U.25.c.6.5.10 was placed at the disposal of the Battalion. A large quantity of salvage was collected while in occupation of this position.	

Morey Major,
Commanding 13th (S) Bn Yorkshire Regiment

Army Form C. 2118.

WAR DIARY
or
INTELLIGENCE SUMMARY.
(Erase heading not required.)

CONFIDENTIAL

WAR DIARY
of
13th (Service) Battalion Yorkshire Regiment

From 1st February 1917.
to 28th February 1917.

(Volume 21).

WAR DIARY
INTELLIGENCE SUMMARY

Place	Date	Hour	Summary of Events and Information	Remarks and references to Appendices
U.28.c.93 Ref Map Special Sh. U.1 to C.6 Scale 1/10000	1st Feb 1918 to 7th Feb 1918		**In the Trenches.** Boundaries as in previous tour. During the tour the climatic conditions were very favourable & the trenches were in a good state of repair. Nightly patrols reconnoitred the enemy wire, no enemy patrols were met. Strong working parties were found by the Support & Reserve Companies & a considerable amount of work was carried out on the improvement of the defences. Enemy artillery on the whole normal. Our artillery were particularly active during the whole tour. On the night of 3rd & 4th Feby inter company relief took place. **Brigade Support.** The usual dispositions were occupied. Working parties were out each night - & erections of wire were constructed & sent up by trench tramway. Whilst in this position abnormal gas shelling took place, the objects being the Batteries in ECOUST	
U.26.c.71 Ref Map Special Sh. U.1 to C.6 Scale 1/10000	7th Feb to 12th Feb 1918			

Army Form C. 2118.

WAR DIARY
or
INTELLIGENCE SUMMARY
(Erase heading not required.)

Instructions regarding War Diaries and Intelligence Summaries are contained in F. S. Regs., Part II. and the Staff Manual respectively. Title pages will be prepared in manuscript.

13th (SERVICE) BATT. YORKS. REGT.
ORDERLY ROOM.

Place	Date	Hour	Summary of Events and Information	Remarks and references to Appendices
A.26.c.11. R.1.M.4. Spruce St. W.1.C.6. Sallyscoo	7th Feb. 1918 8th 9th 10th 11th 12th 13th 14/2/17 1918		Bn. in trenches occupying front line trenches in sector by companies. A day & night of quietness. No casualties	
			On the night of 11th Feb 1918 at Dun arm relieved from the line. The 14th Infantry Bde was relieved by 103 Infantry Bde. the Battn being relieved by 2/5 K.R. (Liverpools) R.V. 6. Coy. the Battn moved to Belfast Camp, Enguillere.	
Belfast Camp Enguillere			While in Corps Reserve very strong working parties were found daily for work on the Corps defence Battn. & Brigade were placed in support of the Bde on the 18th inst. Training and carried out in accordance and Schools for general interest were continued. Training took place in the half days free from work. Events very form of amusement was organised by	

Army Form C. 2118

WAR DIARY
or
INTELLIGENCE SUMMARY.
(Erase heading not required.)

Place	Date	Hour	Summary of Events and Information	Remarks and references to Appendices
BEHNST CAMP ERVILLERS	12th FEB to 28th FEBY 1918		(Contd) a Sports Committee & every endeavour made to afford recreation for the men after the strenuous period in the line. The Division being in Corps Reserve units were ordered to be prepared to move up here upon receipt of notice in case of eventualities. Enemy aeroplanes were on two occasions dropped bombs in the vicinity of the camp without causing any casualties. Owing to the Division would move to GHQ Reserve on 28th but was received on 27th inst. The Batt" moved by route march occupied billets at BIHUCOURT.	

Comdg. 13th (S)/13th Yorkshire Regt.
R M Vines
Lieut-Colonel,

40th Division.
121st Infantry Brigade.

WAR DIARY

13th BATTALION

THE YORKSHIRE REGIMENT

MARCH 1918.

CONFIDENTIAL.

War Diary
of
13th (Service) Battalion Yorkshire Regiment

from March 1st 1918
to March 31st 1918

(VOLUME 22)

WAR DIARY

INTELLIGENCE SUMMARY

Army Form C. 2118.

Place	Date	Hour	Summary of Events and Information	Remarks and references to Appendices
BAILLEULVAL	1st March to 11th March		Every preparation was made for the immediate departure of the Battalion in case of eventualities. In the meantime, however, training was vigorously continued. The attack in conjunction with tanks was practised on the tactical method of training performed. Companies on several occasions visiting the Tank Depot at WAILLY for the purpose. The Corps Commander inspected the Brigade in the neighbourhood of PANSART on the 10th March and expressed congratulations on the good appearance and steadiness of the troops on parade. On the evening of the 11th March an intimation was received for the Brigade to be in readiness to move at 2 hours notice.	
HENDECOURT	12th March to 10th March		This entailing more maneuvres the following day. All surplus kit was dumped and the personnel detailed to remain behind on the going into action were allotted billets in BAILLEUVAL. The Battalion left BAILLEUVAL at 6 p.m. and arrived at No 5 Camp, HENDECOURT at 11 p.m. Tour huts constituted the quarters of the troops. The huts were in good repair and very comfortable. The Baths on BLAIREVILLE were taken full advantage of and the ranges on close proximity to the Camps were most daily. Practices were carried out on the field firing Range at WAILLY the tank depot was again visited on three occasions in order to carry out further demonstrations. The weather was cold but clement these augmenting training and educational efforts. Whilst in the present position the Battalion had to be in readiness to move at 2 hours notice by day and 12 hours notice by night. During the night of the 10th and early hours of the 21st March Enemy Guns Fire could be heard, clearly indicating an intense bombardment of our trench systems on this area.	

WAR DIARY
INTELLIGENCE SUMMARY

(Erase heading not required.)

Army Form C. 2118.

Instructions regarding War Diaries and Intelligence Summaries are contained in F. S. Regs., Part II. and the Staff Manual respectively. Title pages will be prepared in manuscript.

Place	Date	Hour	Summary of Events and Information	Remarks and references to Appendices
ST LEGER B 9 d	21st March		At 6 a.m. signals brought the message "Stand to" and at 7.15 a.m. the Battalion were ordered to leave HENDECOURT and march to HAMELINCOURT whilst on the line of march the Battalion was ordered to proceed across the open from HAMELINCOURT and occupy the front trenches of the 3rd system of defence immediately to the east of ST LEGER with the 18th Suffolk Regt occupying the north trench to the right. The situation was vague as it was not known to what depth the enemy had penetrated. The Battalion proceeded across country in diamond formation. Companies were instructed as follows:— "C" Company on right front to keep in touch with 18th Suffolk Regt on Right. "A" Company on left front to keep in touch with "C" Coy on its Right. Scouts from these two Companies were sent forward and protection of the left flank of "A" Company was provided by a platoon of "D" Company who were the support. "B" Company were in Battalion Reserve. At 6 p.m. Battalion Head Quarters were established in B 9 d with "B" Company close at hand. "D" Company occupied the Army Line astride the SENSEE VALLEY. At 12 midnight a report was received from O.C. "D" Company that it had occupied the front line trenches as ordered after opposition from the enemy. Battalion Head Quarters then moved to the SUNKEN ROAD B 4 b — the Support Company moving to gun-pits in Mt Copse in B 4 t and the Reserve Company to the SUNKEN ROAD at Battalion Head Quarters. It was then found that "A" and "C" Companies had attempted	

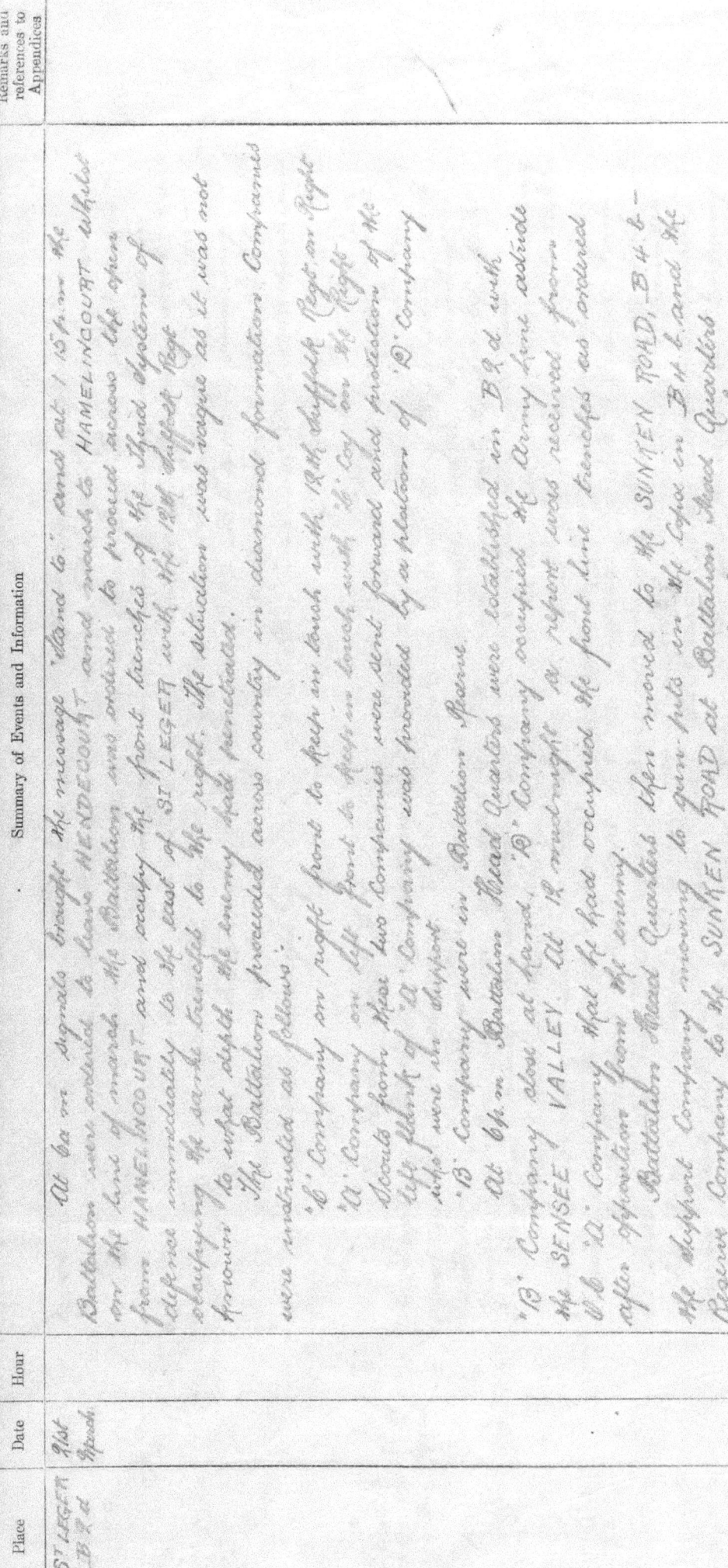

WAR DIARY
or
INTELLIGENCE SUMMARY.

(Erase heading not required.)

Army Form C. 2118.

3

Place	Date	Hour	Summary of Events and Information	Remarks and references to Appendices
ST. LEGER B.2.d	21st March		to secure their trenches by approaching up the C.T. running due east in B.1.b. "A" Company leading. A patrol reported enemy holding the two Companies spotted in the C.T. and B/K C.T. Recd. with a Lewis Gun team, worked his way along the trench and by bombing and Lewis gunning succeeded in killing and dispersing four Machine Gun teams of the enemy and capturing their guns. "B" Coy then proceeded to occupy the front-line trench from the S.B. Wood, B.5.a.40%. running S.S.E. for a distance of 250 yards. "C" Company made several attempts to work along trench to right of "A" Company but were met with machine gun fire.	
ST. LEGER SUNKEN RD B.1.b.	22nd March		At 7a.m. Capt. H. Hampton of "D" Coy with two platoons made a bombing attack on the portion of the trench occupied by the enemy and succeeded in clearing the trench, killing about 40 of the enemy and capturing 7 Machine Guns. Within a few minutes, however, the enemy were counter-attacked in force, estimated at 500 and drove out the party. Capt. H. Hampton being killed and about 68 Wood severely wounded. As it was considered that the portion of the trench in question running from "D" Coys Right flank to the dugouts left at BANKS WOOD should be taken, it was decided to make a frontal attack with the Reserve Company. "B" Company under Capt. R.S. de Quetteville, therefore attacked from the eastern road in B.10.a at 11:45 a.m. attacking to the N.E. along both sides of the ni-entrant. Artillery co-operated. @ 10 minutes 3 howitzer barrage being put on the trench & at barrage then lifting 100 yards and continuing for 15 minutes. During the first barrage the Company advanced within 150 yards of the trench, having covered some 400 yards	

WAR DIARY

or

INTELLIGENCE SUMMARY.

(Erase heading not required.)

Army Form C. 2118.

4

Place	Date	Hour	Summary of Events and Information	Remarks and references to Appendices
ST LEGER SUNKEN ROAD B.4.c.	22nd March		As soon as the barrage lifted the trench was attacked and gained, the General running and unatamly heavy casualties. Touch was then obtained with the 12th Suffolks on the right and the line was complete at 11 noon. Several counter attacks were arranged on this trench by the enemy but were all repulsed with loss to him. Then the left line were in touch with the 9th Bn N.F. 34th Division. At 6.15 p.m Brigade orders were received that in the event of the 34th Division retiring the Battalion would retire gradually to the Army Line. This Division was seen to retire through St LEGER and along the road to the north of it, so it was decided to fall back this was done gradually. B Company covering the retirement and leaving the line about 9.30 p.m — much to their disgust. The enemy by this time had almost completely surrounded this Company and only slight leadership extricated it. Company from a precarious situation. A small portion of the Company was detached by the enemy. On reaching the Army line it was found that the 109th Brigade were not astride the St LEGER - ERVILLERS Road as expected. The Battalion, therefore, took up a position on the Army line with its left flank resting on the ERVILLERS - ST LEGER Road and its right about 600 yards to the S.E. Liaison established by Mr Payton on the left. On the left we were in touch with the 4th Grenadier Guards. Our Right flank was in the air. Patrols to the Right flank reported the line unoccupied for a distance of 1000 yards. The Army line was, in this vicinity, 18" deep and 3' wide and badly sited, the field of view was fire being very restricted. The night of 22nd was spent in consolidating the positions and in patrolling the ground in front of the same.	

WAR DIARY
INTELLIGENCE SUMMARY
(Erase heading not required.)

Army Form C. 2118.

5

Place	Date	Hour	Summary of Events and Information	Remarks and references to Appendices
ERVILLERS B8.c.40.10	March 23rd		On the morning of the 43rd Battalion Head Quarters was established at B8.c.no.10. Hostile machine gun fire shewed the enemy to be some 200 yards from our trenches. A C.T. running from the aerodrome towards 1ST LEGER about the centre of the Battalion front was a source of annoyance as the enemy had occupied it and had established M.G. positions there which, although not affecting our own line seriously, certainly hampered approaches and commanded the line to our left and right. At about 10.30 a.m. the 91st Middlesex Regt formed up on the ST LEGER-ERVILLERS Road with their left flank on our front line trenches and attacked to the S.E. On reaching our fight flank they took up a position on the army line in which with our right flank we were then protected on both flanks and the storage of personnel it had been impossible for the Battalion to be formed in depth. However, two platoons were with drawn and left up a position about 150 yards in rear of front line. Lewis team Guards were also digging in in force some 100 yards still further to the rear. The remainder of the day was quiet. At dusk patrols went out through our wire to obtain knowledge of the enemy's position and to prevent wire-cutting. Enemy was located 150 yards to front except at the Advance Post on C.T. S.A.A. and bombs opportunely arrived and the machine Gunner on the C.T. was put out of action very quickly by a rifle grenade. At 8 p.m. a report was received from the 91st Middlesex Regt on our right that cavalry had approached their line but were driven below of them.	

WAR DIARY

INTELLIGENCE SUMMARY

Army Form C. 2118.

Place	Date	Hour	Summary of Events and Information	Remarks and references to Appendices
ERVILLERS B.8.c.90.10	Aug 27th		At 11 a.m. Brigade Orders were received to the effect that the Battalion would be relieved by the 21st Middlesex Regt side-slipping to the left, the Battalion on relief being ordered to take up a position immediately north of BEHAGNIES. The 21st Middlesex R. however, received different orders and the relief did not take place. The situation remained fairly quiet during the whole of the day. Orders were received at 5 P.M. to arrange with the Irish Guards for that Battalion to relieve us the relief was complete by 10 P.M. on the Companies having reached the road leading from ST LEGER to ERVILLERS when the enemy attacked in force on the front of the 21st Middlesex Regt and to the right of that Battalion. Our Companies immediately re-occupied the line in conjunction with the Irish Guards. The 21st Middlesex Regt retired on the right. 2/Lt L. Ward who commanded the two platoons in support saw that the attack did not immediately concern our front, he therefore advanced from his position at the double and formed a defensive flank on the Battalion Regt flank. As it was found that the enemy were approaching in small numbers along the trench from the right, 2/Lt L. Ward left a small party of Guards and Yorks to meet them under a Guards Sergeant the Sergeant succeeded in bayonetting five of the enemy and bringing in a Staff as prisoner. The two Support Platoons proceeded to dig in a line at right angles to the Army Line and parallel to the ST LEGER-ERVILLERS Road. The Commanding officer of the Irish and Coldstream Guards decided to continue this line 2nd travelled to the road right through to ERVILLERS. This was done. Our Battalion took over 500 yards of frontage with its left flank	

WAR DIARY

INTELLIGENCE SUMMARY

Army Form C. 2118.

Place	Date	Hour	Summary of Events and Information	Remarks and references to Appendices
ERVILLERS B.80.40.10	March 24th		on the strong line and spent the remainder of the night digging in. The night the 4th Middlesex Regt. held from the right of the 2nd Middlesex R to ERVILLERS the Scottish Guards	
	March 26th		The new line was consolidated with a good field of fire and west. ST LEGER-ERVILLERS Road was used as a support line and was held by men of the Welsh and East Surreys of the 12th Brigade. During the morning enemy were seen in the distance on the MORY-ERVILLERS Road also moving in the valley about B.14.d. Artillery were informed of this movement and good shooting was observed. The feature of the day was the excellent shooting by our own Artillery on our own lines the ERVILLERS-ST LEGER Road, our support line, was shelled most persistently and accurately, heavy casualties being caused. Despite numerous messages this continued during the whole day. Captain W Bromilie, R.A.M.C, the Battalion M.O was killed by our own shelling some 300 yards behind our line and 100 yards from the enemy. This shooting was by heavy guns from the direction of HAMELINCOURT. At 6 p.m. the Generals received orders that they were to retire to a line in the vicinity of MOYENVILLE at 8 p.m. It was arranged that the Battalion should retire in conjunction with them. The retirement was carried out in order despite our heavies and the Battalion marched	119

WAR DIARY or INTELLIGENCE SUMMARY

Army Form C. 2118.

Place	Date	Hour	Summary of Events and Information	Remarks and references to Appendices
DOUCHY-les-AYETTE Ref Sheet 51 II	28th March		across country to COURCELLES leaving ETINEHEM on the left. Battalion had got on the left of the position, on the flank and astride from COURCELLES to DOUCHY-les-AYETTE. Doucy Battalion marched to its transport lines near DOUCHY-les-AYETTE, where it was provided for the men.	
BIENVILLERS	29th March		The march was continued at 8.30 a.m. and our destination, BIENVILLERS, reached at midday. The Regimental transport accompanied the Battalion to this place. The traffic passing through the village became very abnormal towards 1 p.m. Artillery, supply columns and representatives of all the mounted services were proceeding into the back areas. The enemy having occupied BIENVILLERS shortly after our arrival. The Rumour for this retirement was that the enemy had reported to have broken through our lines at HEBUTERNE and that cavalry and armoured cars. At 1.30 a.m. the order was received to take up a position on the ridge on the village outskirts. During the course of the afternoon troops moved forward to take up tactical positions and a division of Australians passed forward towards HEBUTERNE. The Battalion was not ordered any further forward, the Regimental transport was told in readiness to depart at 5 minutes notice.	
BAILLEULVAL	8th March		Relief Orders were received at midnight and the Battalion marched to BAILLEULVAL and bivouacked on its outskirts.	
HABARCQ	18th		The following morning, moving after a four hours march, HABARCQ was reached, where billets were provided for a night's sojourn.	
SUS-ST-LEGER	19th		At 9 a.m. on the 19th March the Battalion proceeded to SUS-ST-LEGER. During the evening the transport left behind at BAILLEULVAL prior to the Battalion going into action rejoined.	

Army Form C. 2118.

WAR DIARY
~~INTELLIGENCE SUMMARY.~~
(Erase heading not required.)

Instructions regarding War Diaries and Intelligence Summaries are contained in F. S. Regs. Part II. and the Staff Manual respectively. Title pages will be prepared in manuscript.

Place	Date	Hour	Summary of Events and Information	Remarks and references to Appendices
MARQUAY	March 30th		SUS-ST-LEGER was left at 10 a.m. on the 30th inst. and MARQUAY reached about 4 p.m. on the afternoon. The night was spent here	
NEUF BERQUIN	March 31st		The 40th Division, too Artillery, was transferred from the XIIIth Corps to the XIVth Corps to relieve the 5th Division on the 31st March. The move was carried out by Motor lorries on Brigade Groups. The 119th Brigade entrained on the SAVIE - S.POL Road at 12 noon and proceeded to NEUF BERQUIN via S.POL - LILLERS - ST VENANT - NEUVILLE. Billets were allotted to the Battalion in NEUF BERQUIN	

Nicolui.
Major,
Commanding 19th (W)Bn Yorkshire Regt.

40th Division.
121st Infantry Brigade.

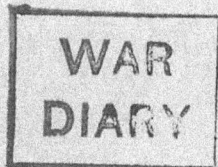

13th BATTALION

YORKSHIRE REGIMENT

APRIL 1 9 1 8

WAR DIARY
or
INTELLIGENCE SUMMARY.
(Erase heading not required.)

Army Form C. 2118.

Place	Date	Hour	Summary of Events and Information	Remarks and references to Appendices
Neuf Berquin	6/4/18		Orders were received that the 4th Division would relieve the 31st Division in the line on the 7th April, 1918.	
Neuf-Berquin	7/4/18		The Battalion moved from NEUF BERQUIN at 9 a.m., halting at SAILLY-SUR-LYS for dinners and tea's and at 6 p.m. proceeded to take over the line. The Battalion took over the left sector of the RGT. BRIGADE sector, boundaries I.31.d..1.9 to I.20.d.4.7.; dispositions, two companies in the line, one in support, and one in reserve.	
	8/4/18		The shelling was negligible at the commencement of the tour, but towards the 5th and 6th of April enemy artillery did a great deal of registering. Our artillery patrols encountered no hostile parties during their nightly reconnaissance. The shelling on the 7th and 8th became more marked clearly indicating an impending raid or attack. At 4.15 a.m. on the 9th April enemy trench mortars, 8 inch, on a howitzer line and in rear – 77 m.m., H.T.'s and a few 5.9", H.E. and gas Hell troops were at once warned to stand to including M.G.'s and Lights T.M.B. At 4.30 the 9th 4.T. on our left were known that the barrage had nothing to do with the supposed raid on the right. The barrage continued from 4.30 to 10.30, and did considerable damage to Rubecillage line between Gout Aver and SHAFTSBURY AVE. At 11.20 a.m. information came from the Brigade that the enemy was through the Regt. Brigade Liaison Post on the Road	

WAR DIARY or INTELLIGENCE SUMMARY

Army Form C. 2118.

Place	Date	Hour	Summary of Events and Information	Remarks and references to Appendices
BOIS GRENIER	9/4/18		Middlesex were holding TIN BARN AVE. The right against SHAFTESBURY AVE as far as 0.25.b.0.0 and extended their right to RED HOUSE POST. "B" company was ordered to man TRAMLINE AVE. which arrows to LA VESEE POST. The front Line companies were informed of the position and ordered to hold on at all costs. The 9th N.F.s were also informed and asked to make a defensive flank along PARK ROW AVE.	
		11.0 A.M.	At 11.0 A.M. the enemy were reported to be at CHAPEL FARM. Orders were given to C Company to hand a platoon through BOIS-GRENIER to get touch with the enemy. At the same time the 9th N.F. reported that they were holding PARK ROW all were extending through LA VESEE to GUNNER POST.	
		11.54 a.m.	At 11.54 a.m. the Colony were reported to be attacking the Right flank Post PETER & PAUL. The S.O.S. was sent up by rifles, verey lights and through the 9th N.F.'s, but no artillery replied. The Maj. and S.M. fired, and the attack was driven off. A strong patrol of enemy attempted to enter the line between PATRICK & PERCY. These also were driven off. At 12 noon the O.C. 2nd Middlesex arrived at ad. Brit. Headquarters and stated that the enemy were then near RED HOUSE FARM and that the battalion had been practically annihilated. At 12.30 p.m. the O.C. left company found these with both flanks in the air, and till no other Middlesex troops except	
			Lt. Tillard + Gun + about 30 a.k. and the enemy were in CULVERT FARM. The Middlesex troops were placed under the command of the O.C. the battalion.	

WAR DIARY or INTELLIGENCE SUMMARY

Army Form C. 2118.

Place	Date	Hour	Summary of Events and Information	Remarks and references to Appendices
BOIS GRENIER	9/4/18		A half company of the Middlesex were ordered to withdraw via the Subsidiary line and Thistle in the line between SHAFTSBURY AVE. and I.19.d.4.9. PETER PAN POST was ordered to withdraw to ST. MARTIN'S LANE, and PENSAM to I.25.d.6.0. The O.C. B company reported that his right flank had been unable to reach RED HOUSE FARM and had taken up time at RIVER LAIES with his right flank in an about I.19.a.3.5. The new station of B company in accordance though LA VESEE towards STREAKY BACON FARM to try + get touch with the 17th Suffolks, who were probably there, whilst the right flank of C company pushed out towards their right for the same purpose. 2nd B.A.L. under 2/Lt. Collins ordered to dig in between junction of TRAMLINE AVE. with Subsidiary Line and LA VESEE POST. At 1.30 a.m. the platoon of D. coy got touch with the 9th A.I. between LA VESEE and GUNNER POST and then pushed on to STREAKY BACON FARM when they got touch with two platoons of the 10th Division. 5 a.m. from then the line was established as follows:- Left by front line held from PAN POST to PETER PAN through THARM ST. to STAM YAY POST thence along CHARING CROSS, SHAFTSBURY AVE, that trench east of SHAFTSBURY HOUSE along line of LAIES to I.13.B.6.1 across LAIES to I.13.C.3.2. thence the 9th N.F. continued it to STREAKY BACON FARM, with one of our platoons established just north of that farm. Supports along TRAMLINE AVE. to I.19.a.9.6. while their right flank rested on 9th R.I.R.	

WAR DIARY
INTELLIGENCE SUMMARY
(Erase heading not required.)

Army Form C. 2118.

Place	Date	Hour	Summary of Events and Information	Remarks and references to Appendices
BOIS GRENIER	9/4/18		Piers pickets were posted in front. BRAZEL FARM was our to RED HOUSE. The latter trough the front line was held by the battalion with half a company of the 2 N. Fus. Meanwhile succeeded 300 yards. This was the line on which it was decided to stand, and orders were given to all companies that it was to be held at all costs. It was held until 4 p.m. not only when SANITARY AVE. fell but orders for the withdrawal sent then in the to the land. The oblivious post at PEACH BARN was kept manned continuously and gave valuable information as to the enemy's movements. This was forwarded by pigeon whilst they lasted and through the 9th N. Fus., but no answers were ever received and not artillery assistance was given.	
		3.30 p.m.	At 3.30 p.m. the enemy were seen to be massing about I 31. b. Centrals, the artillery were informed. About 4 p.m. Y. b. Fifth Suffolk, there was an organised rifle grenade bombardment and the 2 N. Fus., who opened the getting position and fire on the enemy.	
		4.30 p.m.	At 4.30 p.m. the enemy commenced to be giving back to their men from line, a movement of about 30 being noticed.	
		7.30	At 7.30 p.m. the enemy attacked TERRY POST, in two parties of 40 each. At 8.30 p.m. the attack was taken up and the enemy was driven out of our front line with Rifle Fire, Rifle grenades and a Stokes gun. The Stokes	

WAR DIARY or INTELLIGENCE SUMMARY.

(Erase heading not required.)

Army Form C. 2118.

Place	Date	Hour	Summary of Events and Information	Remarks and references to Appendices
BOIS GRENIER	9/4/18	2 p.m. (Approx)	men had been kept in readiness for this attack, it found it worn out and apparently had slightly bad luck until to admit which it then freed. The weight passed without incident. 6.20 Ramir from Return were divided amongst all troops in the sector, which amounted to approximately 300 including M.G.C., L.T.M. and 2nd Middlesex. Hot tea was served to all troops before dawn and additional ammunition got up from the 9th N.H.Q. Reserve. Satchels were filled out all night.	
		dawn	At 9.30 a.m. orders were received that the Battalion was under the command of O.C. 103rd Bde.	
	10/4/18 2 a.m.		At 2 a.m. Patrols were sent out from A, C & B companies reporting to get back information. They on their run to detect enemy's renewed attack. The enemy were holding RED HOUSE POST thence along the Redline Camouflage, thence MORT FARM AVE. to CULVERT FARM F 6 1 3 4 centred to 1.3.1 In central where is this the front line in front of PATROK POST and that they were digging in on the line.	
		8 p.m. to 10 a.m.	At 8.45 a.m. the enemy attacked PATRICK POST and was repulsed. At 10 a.m. a heavy T.M. from MONT FARM fired on the junction of SHAFTSBURY AVE. and the Dubbing line, a direct hit on our blocking post arising below annihilated the garrison of the post.	

WAR DIARY or INTELLIGENCE SUMMARY

Place	Date	Hour	Summary of Events and Information	Remarks and references to Appendices
BOIS GRENIER	10/4/16		B.H.Q. being the cut through the east wall of SHAFTESBURY AVE. at I.25.c.8.9. Only a similarity in the dubsideway dam about I.19.c.8.1. and no communication was maintained with A Company in SHAFTESBURY AVE. as the trench junction was impassable and completely dominated by enemy machine gun fire. One block in the dubsideway dam was now being made place at about 50 to 100 yards in rear of SHAFTESBURY AVE.	
		10.15 a.m.	At 10.15 a.m. the enemy was reported to be massing in front I.31.d. & I.30.a. & the 9 & 2 M.G.s were reported at this, and they moved their Batt.Q. from I.30.a. S.E. to RUE FLEURIE POST before dawn on the 10th inst., as all our Orderly Room work etc. was sent along to their old B.H.Q. with the Assistant Adjutant, a telephone line was laid there and the 9 & M.G. connected up from there to their B.H.Q.	
		1 p.m.	At 1 p.m. the enemy attacked between JOCK'S J.Y. and PERCY POST, about 150 of the enemy forces their way into HAYMARKET and took in temporarily post between a cpl. & the my. it and to try on the left. A Lewis was established along old french trench from LONDON BRIDGE to TRAMLINE AVE. about I.20.c. & I.20.d. PERCY POST held out also post west JOCK'S J.Y. and the enemy were driven out of HAYMARKET.	

Army Form C. 2118.

WAR DIARY
or
INTELLIGENCE SUMMARY.
(Erase heading not required.)

Place	Date	Hour	Summary of Events and Information	Remarks and references to Appendices
BOIS GRENIER	19/4/18		Up to this date the enemy attempts of intercepting has been of trained. Mjr. L.R. 21 Regt. and Adj of Regt.	
		7 p.m.	The enemy was still massed outside HAZEBROUCK, and A + B companies were ordered to attack and drive them back. The attack to be launched by two strong parties advancing from RUE JUNIOR STONE and RUE DE LONDON BRIDGE and TITI RAVINE to take place about 4 p.m. Field to withdraw and receive from the 103rd Brigade a	
		3.20	reinforcement of a Bn of the 6.6th of the 21st Middlesex, 13 of when 9 R.W.Fs and no at RUE FLEURIE POST, No. 11 Suffolks holding the line from LA ROLANDERIE FARM to their right. Flank forms and the enemy returning on ERQUINGHEM. Under these circumstances it was decided that the 7 Kings OYLI would move HALF WAY HOUSE ahead at once move to an ADVANCED FARM and hold the above notice viaducy E MAIN A ROBERTIETE ROAD. The 13th Yorks to withdraw first leaving along ???? and flank guards in SHAFTSBURY AVE and front lines only at H.Q. and half to my their in such as moved out at one under Capt. de Quetteville had orders by H.Q. known to move out above. Remainder of Coys of H battalion to remain with the RUE MARLE since done by Lt Colonel Brug. Headly being ?????? to concentrate at TOUQUET FARM ENTIER. Same to with ??? 1.15 of John ? 22???.	

D.D.&I., London, E.C.
(Army) W1 W1777/M2031 750,000 5/17 Sch. 52 Forms/C.2118/14

Army Form C. 2118.

WAR DIARY
or
INTELLIGENCE SUMMARY.
(Erase heading not required.)

Place	Date	Hour	Summary of Events and Information	Remarks and references to Appendices
BOIS GRENIER	19/4/15	4.45 p.m.	9th N.Z. Division with Lincolns, Tynesiders, R.F., R. Iniskilling Fusiliers, Hants etc. The Brigade wounded. Attack was covered.	
		5 a.m.	The enemy reached SHAFTSBURY AVE. and a line remnants fell back on TRAMLINE AVE. which became our front line at 5.54 a.m. which withdrawal commenced and was quietly swallowed by the mist.	
			At 5.30 p.m. all our companies had reached RUE FREURIE POST Enemy RUE MARIE. The enemy machine gun not all across Track D. On approaching Futterville deployed and advanced to attack of about 500 yards away. Apparently any way bank of fire was well aimed at 4.43. At 4.45 a.m. 7th Battn H.Q. the whole Battalion in the ESPLANADES – ARMENTIERES ROAD. At RABLA ... Rue Fort MARIETTE now their day and the companies halted in the latter bridge. The leading platoons of ...	
TOUQUET PARMENTIER			If y walled on the 4th A.A. Batteries. A Officer was killed and the patrol which was driven off but 7 o'n of the D.B.N.R. came to O.P.L.S. by the factory bridge the 103rd Infantry Fired, commanded or were received to take over at the request of Railway came over level crossing at B 21. a. 13. 5 at 17.23 to 20. A ...	

WAR DIARY or INTELLIGENCE SUMMARY

Army Form C. 2118.

Place	Date	Hour	Summary of Events and Information	Remarks and references to Appendices
FAUQUET PARMENTIER	10/4/18		own followed up at anything but owing to the darkness of the night it was impossible to ascertain all of the time.	
	11/4/18		The C.O. went round the Outposts at dawn and found it very congested with troops. He sent the C.O.s of the 13 Gloucesters & our left and 11 Suffolks on right and they agreed to our withdrawal to support at 7.30 am. The Brigade were written to for instructions.	
		8am from 4am	At 7am the Battalion moved into support at Pont D'ACHELLES and dug a number of straggling supports. From THE DUNE and again through the left flank was surrendered. These stragglers were collected and sent back to it. The 11 counter attack was brought against ROMARIN. The 12 E. Suffolks were in front and the 13 Gloucesters in close support. In reserve of some yards we made at 2.00 pm orders were received not to press the attack as Troops were to be withdrawn at night.	
PONT D'ACHELLES		4pm	Orders were received to withdraw the 13 Gloucesters to provide a screen to enable the 12 E. Suffolks to get through.	
		5.30pm At 11.30pm	The Battalion withdrew and marched to a field on the BAILLEUL ROAD north of LA CRECHE and took up position in outpost along the BAILLEUL Main Road.	

WAR DIARY or INTELLIGENCE SUMMARY

Army Form C. 2118.

Place	Date	Hour	Summary of Events and Information	Remarks and references to Appendices
STRAZEELE	14/4/18	4 a.m.	At 4.00 a.m. this day orders were received with direction to march to STRAZEELE. The Battalion moved off at 5 a.m. marching via BAILLEUL OUTSTREENE and MERRIS.	
		1.30 p.m.	Total orders were received to dig in covering from STRAZEELE to PRADELLES, on brigade frontage. This was difficult as enemy aircraft and enemy of the enemy was active. Patrols were sent out, but no sign by night the position being too exposed in front of the railway between	
		8 a.m.	Patrols were out all day. Started a series of Australian troops on our right flank. Line of the enemy was unknown. Orders were received to move to position of assembly at CROIX ROUGE and thence at 5 p.m. the Battalion marches to BAVINCOVE. The night at was spent in Billeting and the following morning at 9 a.m. a Battalion parade was held notifying will and billets. Names of men were taken down, strength etc. In the light many orders were received. The programme from the Battalion had a certain pretext of be offered once it was reported to the H.Q. and a copy of the Yproles Regs. In accordance with this under the following day the officers and men who formed up for the occasion	

D. D. & L., London, E.C.
(A601) Wt. W1.77/M1291 750,000 5/17 Sch. 52 Forms/C2118/14

Army Form C. 2118.

WAR DIARY
or
INTELLIGENCE SUMMARY.
(Erase heading not required.)

Instructions regarding War Diaries and Intelligence Summaries are contained in F. S. Regs., Part II. and the Staff Manual respectively. Title pages will be prepared in manuscript.

Place	Date	Hour	Summary of Events and Information	Remarks and references to Appendices
ST MARTIN-AU-LAERT.	19/9/15		The 121st Bde was formed within the XIth of the 1st Composite Brigade, 40th Division. The Battalion was supposed temporarily by one company of the 13th Bn East Surrey Regt., and one company of the 2nd East Middlesex Regt. The Composite Brigade moved to the vicinity of the village. There was nothing that warranted in the movements but OUDEZEELE. Tent accommodation was being erected. While in the position strong working parties were found for work in digging the HERZEELE line.	
PROVEN	2/10/15 to 29/11/18		Verbal orders were received that the Battalion was to move in the vicinity of POPERINGHE as immediate the Battalion moving to cover its own post in the time retained. During the dig the water was to be carried out in the WATOU area.	

Lieut. Colonel,
Comdg. 13th Bn. York. Regt.

25TH DIVISION
74TH INFY BDE

13TH BN YORKSHIRE REGT
JLY 1918
(SERVING IN U.K.)

(40 Div
121 Bde June 1916)

Army Form C. 2118.

13TH (S) BATTALION.
YORKSHIRE REGT.

WAR DIARY
or
INTELLIGENCE SUMMARY.
(Erase heading not required.)

Instructions regarding War Diaries and Intelligence Summaries are contained in F. S. Regs., Part II. and the Staff Manual respectively. Title pages will be prepared in manuscript.

Place	Date	Hour	Summary of Events and Information	Remarks and references to Appendices

CONFIDENTIAL

War Diary
of
13th (Service) Battalion Yorkshire Regiment
From 1st May
to

WAR DIARY
INTELLIGENCE SUMMARY

(Erase heading not required.)

Army Form C. 2118.

13TH (S) BATTALION.
YORKSHIRE REGT.

Instructions regarding War Diaries and Intelligence Summaries are contained in F. S. Regs., Part II. and the Staff Manual respectively. Title pages will be prepared in manuscript.

Place	Date	Hour	Summary of Events and Information	Remarks and references to Appendices
PROVEN	1st May		The work on the WATOU line progressed normally, doing nothing parties being furnished daily by each Battalion of the Brigade. During our stay here the enemy seemed to check our bombing enemy the enemy of the PROVEN daily causing the exodus of the majority of the civilian residents.	
OUDEZEELE Rd.	2nd May		On the evening of the 2nd May orders were received to move back to the RYVELD area. The Battalion was clear of PROVEN by 8 a.m. and reached OUDEZEELE, where tent accommodation had been allotted, at 11.45 a.m., marching via WATOU and WINNEZEELE	
KINDERBEUCK	3rd May		Tents were struck at 9.30 a.m. the following morning and conveyed by lorry to the ST MOMELIN Area the advance party also	

WAR DIARY
or
INTELLIGENCE SUMMARY.

(Erase heading not required.)

Army Form C. 2118.

13TH (S) BATTALION,
YORKSHIRE REGT.

Place	Date	Hour	Summary of Events and Information	Remarks and references to Appendices
KINDERBELCK	3rd May		Proceeded to the Area to which the Battalion the two parties of the Battalion arrived OUDEZEELE were left at 1.15 pm. The day was very hot and the many halts caused by the moving column was a great annoyance. In addition a heavy enemy shell transport was moving forward out of our lines had to be made. The Battalion ferried out 5 pm for tea. The march was resumed at 6 pm. and KINDERBELCK, the assumed Company area, was reached at 8 p.m. The following movement attempts in 40th Divisional Review were pushed on 3rd May 1918:- "1919 - AWARDS:- Under authority granted by His Majesty the King, the VI Corps Commander has awarded MILITARY MEDALS to the M.C.O. and	

WAR DIARY
INTELLIGENCE SUMMARY
(Erase heading not required.)

Army Form C. 2118.

13TH (S) BATTALION.
YORKSHIRE REGT.

Place	Date	Hour	Summary of Events and Information	Remarks and references to Appendices
KINDERBECK	May		"Men turned in the lorrowed with "Part Route Orders" then the day for "duration to duty on patrol "Contact displays among the return "Operations undertaken by the Division between 21st and 26th March, 1918.	

Honorary Medals

xxx   xxx   xxx

295/A Serjt   J Wheatley   13th Yorkshire Regiment
34104 Cpl (L/Sergt) A Hogg   "
12033 Corpl   A F Hopper   "
21214 Private A W Bowles   "
       "   B Eccles   "
14408 Pte (A/C) A Cooper   "
12487 Private J Popples   "
24889   "   J Adams   "
23437   "   J Kenny   "
28030   "   W Allworthy   "
21845   "   J B Ampton   "

List of Casualties attached

Army Form C. 2118.

18TH (S) BATTALION.
YORKSHIRE REGT.

No. ....
Date ....

WAR DIARY
or
INTELLIGENCE SUMMARY.

(Erase heading not required.)

Instructions regarding War Diaries and Intelligence Summaries are contained in F. S. Regs., Part II. and the Staff Manual respectively. Title pages will be prepared in manuscript.

Place	Date	Hour	Summary of Events and Information	Remarks and references to Appendices
KINDERBECK	1st May		Major General Greenly, C.B, C.M.G, D.S.O. Commanding the Division, addressed the Officers & N.C. Officers at a ceremonial Parade of the whole Brigade held on the Morning of the 1st May. He had been formerly with the Division; has now returned to the Division; having assumed Command of the Battalion and Quarters now being prepared to him as instructed, went to be despatched to the Base. The orders have been temporarily suspended for the 26th April & this may possibly be received to the effect that the movement of the Battalion should be proceeded with at once. The return of the following Officers to a Battalion showing the Military Command of their Grade Mother J. McGeorge M.C. was not attached (See Appendix A)	

D.D. & L. London, E.C. (A8001) Wt. W17171/M2031 750,000 5/17 Sch. 52 Forms/C2118/14

Army Form C. 2118.

18TH (S) BATTALION,
YORKSHIRE REGT.

WAR DIARY
or
INTELLIGENCE SUMMARY.
(Erase heading not required.)

Place	Date	Hour	Summary of Events and Information	Remarks and references to Appendices
KINDERBECK	4th to 9th May		M.T. Stores, Motorcycles, Equipment etc. Surplus to W.E. and handed over to be returned to DADOS as Machinery no possible. On the 6th May. The advanced of the Battalion Surplus proceeded to the Base Depot CALAIS. entraining at ST OMER Station at 5pm. The Regimental Transport did not proceed with the party but remained in the location pending disposal.	
OUDEZEELE	10th May		On the morning of the 10th May the Battalion [Heavy Draft?] together with the advanced detachment of transport proceeded and [concentrated?] in the neighbourhood of OUDEZEELE, Lookery and OOST HOECK. BN H.Q's WEMAERS CAPPEL - LE BONNET. THE Surplus Half H.Q's - WEMAERS CAPPEL - LE BONNET THE Surplus	

WAR DIARY
or
INTELLIGENCE SUMMARY.

(Erase heading not required.)

Army Form C. 2118.

13TH (S) BATTALION
YORKSHIRE REGT.

Place	Date	Hour	Summary of Events and Information	Remarks and references to Appendices
KINDERBECK	10th May		Transport remained at KINDERBECK.	
OUDEZEELE	11th May		A number of N.C.O's and men who were on the Nucleus at the 39th Infantry Base and who were reported to the Battalion having been struck off strength of Nucleus of the Battalion and (Brigade) Head Quarters, for rejoining the Battalion was reported, met the Battalion having gone up near the front line trenches on relief of Canadian Division for the working & carrying & general duties of between two lines and coming for Rest and recommending of water, rations and Branches in the support line. The whole Battalion on the line was relieved in sequence at the time was also withdrawing in sequence at the time of our late attack, so that on the event of our late attack, so that no re-considerable but troops would really to the Rear (nearer already suffered heavy to those trenches newly dug with every unit to the front of mens moved with every	

WAR DIARY or INTELLIGENCE SUMMARY

13TH (S) BATTALION YORKSHIRE REGT.

Army Form C. 2118.

Place	Date	Hour	Summary of Events and Information	Remarks and references to Appendices
OUDEZEELE	11th to 31st May		A Generation complete as regards transport during August here. Portion of MOs and horses of 1 Commander. On the 11th May the Anglais Regiment transport proceeded to the Base Depot, ETAPLES for transport to complete transport. Further records in connection with the operations undertaken by the Division between the 10th and 26th March may be the 10th Divisional Records traced by the 13th (Service) Coy. of which a written traces of him. — 1966 - Inchiviene Anniv. Army Authority furnished by His Majesty the King. He held the ceremony - certified. the officers and other Ranks who are all not wounded with Divisional	

WAR DIARY
INTELLIGENCE SUMMARY

Army Form C. 2118.

13th (S) BATTALION YORKSHIRE REGT.

Place	Date	Hour	Summary of Events and Information	Remarks and references to Appendices
OUDEZEELE HUTS	1st to 31st May		Routine orders the day for Airmen to duty and generally employed during the whole Minimum month taken by the Division between 21st and 28th March 1918. xxx xxx xxx xxx xxx The Distinguished Service Order /Capt R/ by Mr Greenwell - 13th Yorkshire Regiment The Military Cross /Capt E M Robinson - 13th Yorkshire Regt /2nd Lieut to W Tunnicliff - 13th Yorkshire Regiment The Distinguished Conduct Medal Private W. Robert M.M. - 13th Yorkshire Regiment W Gardner — do — 23107 Private W. H. — do — 119/9 R Rawson 19/63	

WAR DIARY or INTELLIGENCE SUMMARY.

Army Form C. 2118.

13TH (S) BATTALION
YORKSHIRE REGT.

Place	Date	Hour	Summary of Events and Information	Remarks and references to Appendices
OUDEZEELE	11th May to 31st May		The situation in front of the Brigade Frontage was steadily returned during the Month. The Awards received by the Division during the operations undertaken by the Division between the 9th and 13th April 1918 were now published in N.Y. Divisional Routine Orders. The following is a List of recipients in Platoon details:— The Military Cross — (A/Capt) G. Ducker — Yorkshire Regiment (T.F.) attached 13th Battalion. — 13th Yorkshire Regt. 2/Lieut. A. Marsh — 13th Yorkshire Regt. The Distinguished Conduct Medal Serjt. G.S. Metcalfe — 13th Yorkshire Regt. 10.11.96	

WAR DIARY
or
INTELLIGENCE SUMMARY.
(Erase heading not required.)

Army Form C. 2118.

13TH (S) BATTALION,
YORKSHIRE REGT.

Place	Date	Hour	Summary of Events and Information	Remarks and references to Appendices
UDRELEUX			**The Military Medal** — 13th Yorkshire Regt.	
			Nº 33173 Sgt A Anton — 13th Yorkshire Regt.	
			12599 " H Clarke — do —	
			18516 Cpt R Grover — do —	
			16414 A/C A Shenko — do —	
			29543 Pte H Ball — do —	
			39182 A/C L Jackson — do —	
			23-90 Pte J Mellotte — do —	
			24143 " J M Gott — do —	
			29554 " J Ball — do —	
			24148 A/C A Smith — do —	
			235633 Pte A Roots — do —	
			A Warrant this was issued to the 30th July 1917, the Battalion is shortly to proceed to H.Q. shortly would shortly be transferred	
			J. M. Duncan	
			Comdg. Williams Lieut.-Colonel 13th (SERVICE) Bn. YORKSHIRE REGT.	

13th (SERVICE) Bn. YORKSHIRE REGT.

APPENDIX 'A'
issued with War Diary for May 1918

	Officers	W.O.s	St Sgts and Sergeants	R & F	Total
Head Quarters:-					
Commanding Officer	1				1
Adjutant	1				1
Quarter Master	1				1
Lewis Gun Officer	1				1
Scout Officer	1				1
Sergeant Major		1			1
Qr Mr Sergeant		1			1
Q M Storemen				3	3
Orderly Room Clerk				1	1
Police				1	1
Signalling Officer	1				1
Sergt Instructors:-					
Musketry			5		5
P. & B.T.			1		1
Lewis Gun			2		2
Bomb			1		1
Gas Personnel			1		1
Cook				1	1
Transport:-					
Drivers, 1st line				2	2
Water duties				1	1
Sanitary Duties				1	1
Batmen				6	6
Grooms				2	2
Arm S Sgt (attached)			1		1
Total Headquarters (including attached)	6	2	11	18	37

Appendix "A" continued.   Sheet 2

	Officers	W.O's.	St Sgts and Sergeants	R & F	Total
Company:-					
Officer	1				1
C.S.M.		1			1
C.Q.M.S.			1		1
Gas Personnel (a)				1	1
L.G. Instructors			1		1
Batman				1	1
	1	1	2	2	6

Transport.

Horses.				Vehicles	Bicycles
R	L.D	H.D	Total		
7	3	2ˣ	12	1 Cart, Water 1 Cart, Mess 1 G.S. Wagon (attached from A.S.C.)	3

ˣ Two H.D. Horses attached from A.S.C.

Army Form C. 2118.

WAR DIARY
or
INTELLIGENCE SUMMARY.

(Erase heading not required.)

CONFIDENTIAL

War Diary
-of-
13th (Service) Battalion Yorkshire Regiment

July 1st 1918
to
July 31st 1918.

Army Form C. 2118.

WAR DIARY
or
INTELLIGENCE SUMMARY
(Erase heading not required.)

Place	Date	Hour	Summary of Events and Information	Remarks and references to Appendices
Frinkept Camp Tandsongh	1st to 18th July		The Battalion Training Cadre was carrying on England was stationed at Frinkept Camp, Fandborough, preparatory to proceeding to the Eastern Command to assist in the formation of the new Battalion. During the sojourn here the General Officer commanding the Aldershot Command inspected the Battalion Training Cadre of the Division. All Officers and men were granted seven days leave whilst stationed here	
Aldeburgh Suffolk	20th to 31st July		On the 19th July, in accordance with a movement order received from Brigade, the Training Cadre proceeded to Aldeburgh, Suffolk. On arrival it was found that the formation of the new unit had already commenced. – Strength 13 officers 58 Other Ranks. The organization of the Battalion was	

Army Form C. 2118.

WAR DIARY
or
INTELLIGENCE SUMMARY

(Erase heading not required.)

Instructions regarding War Diaries and Intelligence Summaries are contained in F. S. Regs., Part II. and the Staff Manual respectively. Title pages will be prepared in manuscript.

Place	Date	Hour	Summary of Events and Information	Remarks and references to Appendices
Aldershot Suffolk	17th to 31st July		regimental continued. On the 31st July the total strength was 28 Officers 101 Other Ranks	

✕ Mision
Winston

Lieut-Colonel,
Comdg 13th Yorkshire Regiment.

www.ingramcontent.com/pod-product-compliance
Lightning Source LLC
Chambersburg PA
CBHW080853230426
43662CB00013B/2091